VICT🅝RY
SINGLENESS

The Negro National Anthem

Lift every voice and sing
Till earth and heaven ring,
Ring with the harmonies of Liberty;
Let our rejoicing rise
High as the listening skies,
Let it resound loud as the rolling sea.
Sing a song full of the faith that the dark past has taught us,
Sing a song full of the hope that the present has brought us,
Facing the rising sun of our new day begun
Let us march on till victory is won.

So begins the Black National Anthem, by James Weldon Johnson in 1900. Lift Every Voice is the name of the joint imprint of The Institute for Black Family Development and Moody Press, a division of the Moody Bible Institute.

Our vision is to advance the cause of Christ through publishing African-American Christians who educate, edify, and disciple Christians in the church community through quality books written for African-Americans.

The Institute for Black Family Development is a national Christian organization. It offers degreed and nondegreed training nationally and internationally to established and emerging leaders from churches and Christian organizations. To learn more about The Institute for Black Family Development write us at:

The Institute for Black Family Development
15151 Faust Ave.
Detroit, Michigan 48223

Moody Press, a ministry of Moody Bible Institute,
is designed for education, evangelization, and edification.
If we may assist you in knowing more about Christ
and the Christian life, please write us without obligation:

Moody Press
c/o Moody Literature Ministries
820 N. LaSalle Blvd.
Chicago, Illinois 60610

VICT⊙RY SINGLENESS

A Strategy for Emotional Peace

VALERIE CLAYTON
WITH JEROME CLAYTON

*All descriptions
of the people in this book are fictitious.
The names were selected randomly.
The various descriptions and situations
are used solely to provide an example and
to make the topic discussed applicable to real-life circumstances.
Any similarities to anyone either dead or alive is unintentional.
As for personal examples from our lives,
the names and circumstances were altered for purposes of privacy.*

Library of Congress Cataloging-in-Publication Data

Clayton, Valerie, 1955–
    Victory in singleness : a strategy for emotional peace / Valerie & Jerome Clayton.
        p. cm.
    Includes bibliographical references (p.).
    ISBN 0-8024-4015-0
    1. Single people—Religious life. 2. Emotions—Religious aspects—Christianity. I. Clayton, Jerome, 1962– II. Title.

BV4596.S5 C58 2002
248.8'432—dc21

                                                                2001055834

3 5 7 9 10 8 6 4 2

Printed in the United States of America

CONTENTS

SECTION 2—DISCOURAGEMENT

SECTION 3—BITTERNESS

ACKNOWLEDGMENTS

We thank our Lord and Savior Jesus Christ who never let the dream of this book leave our spirits. He gave us the wisdom, words, and strength to complete this project.

My beloved husband and coauthor, Jerome. Without his support, encouragement, and prayers, none of this would have been possible. He has shown me how to love without expectation, to apply grace and mercy to everyone, and to pray without ceasing. I love you, Jerome, with all of my heart.

We thank our families: Our loving mothers, Hazel and Velma, who have always given us their very best and have taught us how to persist in the face of adversity. Dennis, my beloved father, who took the word "step" out of our relationship and always treated my sister and me like daughters. Daddy (Johnny Sr.), thank you for giving me a special gift, fishing, that has kept me going no matter what. Our brothers and sisters who have helped shape whom we have become: Gayle, Johnny, Jeffrey, Janine, Joseph, Jennifer, Joy, Tineka, Mark, Antonio, and Larry . . . we love you all. We want to acknowledge my late father, Cyril Alvin Sobers, a brilliant man and loving father who passed away when I was a little girl . . . he was my heart. Much thanks to Aunt Evelyn and Uncle Freddie who were always there for us after Daddy died. Uncle Rufus, Aunt Janet, Uncle Al, and Aunt Daphne, thank you for being wonderful godparents.

Faithful Central Bible Church, our spiritual home and refuge, under the faithful leadership of Pastor Kenneth C. Ulmer, who leads his flock by example and constantly encourages us to stretch forth and fulfill our purpose. In particular, we would like to thank Pastor Mary Alice Haye and all the members of the Marriage Works ministry for their prayers, love, and support. We are grateful to Joanne Sanders and the Faithful Central Prayer Team for covering this project with prayer.

Special thanks to our wonderful agent Janet Kobobel Grant of *Books and Such* (e-mail address: jkgbooks@aol.com), who has supported us in our writing endeavors. We greatly appreciate your faith in us.

This book has had special cheerleaders along the way: LisaLisa, Sharon, Madeline, Carolyn, Theresa, Sheryl, MiChelle, Crystel and Kevin, Deidra and James, David and Camille, Stan and Terri, Will and Gala, Steven and Pandora, Gwennie and Kenny. A great big thanks to our critique group. We appreciate all for your fantastic comments: Andrea, Venessa, Tina, Tinisha, Yvette, Sonya, Pandora, Dionne, and Krishna.

Thanks to those who have encouraged us and lead the way: Dr. Ronn Elmore and Dr. LaVerne Tolbert.

Thank you Al and Hattie Hollingsworth who helped us take that Vertical Leap. They have demonstrated what is possible when you dream and persist until you succeed. Frank and Bunny Wilson of Fellowship West, thank you for sharing the secrets of having a successful marriage and investing yourselves in our lives. Thank you Pastor Ed Smith of Zoe Church of Whittier. Many years ago you faithfully taught the Zoe Leadership Class and took the time to answer my question about how to hear the voice of God. You changed my life. Thank you Michael Levin, you were my first writing teacher at the UCLA Writers Extension, and you were a tremendous encouragement.

None of this would have been possible if it were not for Moody Bible Institute who published this work. We greatly appreciate your faith in us.

Very sincerely,
Jerome and Valerie

INTRODUCTION

Thank you for taking time to read this introduction. So many times we skip the first few pages in our eagerness to get to the body of the book. However, by reading this introduction, you will grasp the background and tone of this book.

Victory in Singleness: A Strategy for Emotional Peace is written for the woman who struggles with the negative thoughts and emotions that often accompany prolonged singleness. This book is for the woman who is searching for viable solutions to her real-life hurts so she can become all God has called her to be.

So many women believe that marriage is the solution to wholeness. It is not! Marriage was not designed to meet our *fundamental* emotional needs nor to fill our spiritual void—only God can do that. Yet we entangle ourselves emotionally and spiritually in unhealthy relationships when singleness is viewed as an undesirable state. *Victory in Singleness* is for the unmarried woman who craves victory over her thoughts and emotions. This book deals with root issues that make us want to act ugly. It's all about recognizing, naming, and solving some emotional mess that causes us to make poor choices that lead to despair and hopelessness.

SHACKLED TO BAGGAGE

When we deal with envy, discouragement, and bitterness, it's like dragging around heavy baggage. As we travel through life, we accumulate a variety of experiences: many are lonely, some are disappointing, and others are shameful. As a result, some of us have been pulling around bags jam-packed with envy, others are hauling suitcases full of discouragement, and many have been dragging footlockers crammed with bitterness. All of this is emotional and spiritual baggage. The good news is that through the power of God, we can get rid of these burdens that have weighed us down. We can have the victory because Jesus died to set us free. We can get rid of envy, discouragement, and bitterness.

Envy, discouragement, and bitterness are by no means solely a Black issue or an affliction that occurs only in single women. These feelings are manifestations of a spiritual problem. They come as a result of being human. Any man or woman, single or married, can glean solutions to envy, discouragement, and bitterness by reading this book. However, we wrote this book primarily for Black women because an amazing 60 percent[1] are unmarried. That means that the majority of Black women are single.

LEARNING TO BE FREE

I wasn't one of the fortunate ones who loved being single. My forty-year season of singleness was a roller-coaster ride because I was not at peace. No one told me how to get rid of the baggage. I didn't know what to do with the envy I had towards others, the discouragement I felt believing that my life would never change, the bitterness from previous relationships, or the resulting anger I sometimes felt toward God. The good news is I didn't stay in that condition. I made a decision to change my point of view. I decided I wanted victory over my thoughts and emotions.

I learned strategic moves that:

- changed my thought patterns that led to discouragement,
- transformed bitterness from the past,
- rid myself of envy,
- eliminated fear-driven behavior, and
- got me off of those emotional treadmills.

The biggest lesson I learned was that God was "for" me and not against me. I had an adversarial relationship with God; I believed that I had to wrestle blessings from Him. Once I discovered that God, through His Son Jesus, truly loved me—I had to learn how to walk with confidence in His love for me.

The birthing process of *Victory in Singleness* has been a struggle. There have been times I wanted to give up, not believing that this book would ever be finished. But always, my heart would be drawn back to this project. In retrospect, I realize that many parts of this book could not be written when I desired, because I had yet to: (1) learn the lessons that needed to be taught and (2) meet and marry the coauthor.

My husband is a unique man, a pre-licensed psychotherapist, whose heart is "tuned-in" to the heart of the single Black woman. He has over fifteen years of counseling experience and wisdom beyond his years. Like myself, he prayed many years to meet and marry his mate. He too knows what it takes to wait for what God has for you. This book was written by both of us.

To journey with God on this glorious, yet challenging, adventure, you have to travel light—that means you have to get rid of some baggage. By applying the contents of this book, you can rid yourself of the weights of envy, discouragement, and bitterness and obtain victory while you are single.

FREEDOM FROM TRAPPED THINKING

Victory in Singleness is about changing your focus—from looking at your circumstances to exploring who God created you to be. This book is about the good news that Jesus wants to, and will, give you the victory. A crucial component needed to obtain victory is learning how to control the way we think. When our thinking becomes filled with defeated or incorrect beliefs, we develop what we call "trapped thinking." Trapped thinking is a cyclical system of harmful thoughts about ourselves, our situation, or God that perpetuate envy, discouragement, and bitterness. Therefore, to combat these thoughts, "Free Yourself from Trapped Thinking" chapters are threaded throughout the book. These chapters are dedicated to exposing the thought patterns that keep us bound and providing solutions that will help us walk into freedom from envy, discouragement, and bitterness.

There is only one way to get rid of our baggage: by learning what God says about the circumstance, believing His Word, and applying it to our life. God has empowered each of us to take control over the way we think. We do that by remembering what God says about us, thereby challenging the thoughts that have led to envy, discouragement, and bitterness. In other words, we will learn to put a halt to the lies that we have believed about God (e.g., that He is ignoring us, that He disapproves of us, that He is unfair, that He doesn't care about our circumstances) by discovering what God says about us, understanding His intentions toward us, and applying those principles to our lives.

The "Free Yourself from Trapped Thinking" chapters will help you gain your freedom by teaching you how to apply a strategy that leads to peace. Instead of giving in to envy, you will discover how to take every thought captive, making it obedient to Christ (2 Corinthians 10:5); instead of surrendering to discouragement, you will learn how to be transformed by the renewing of your mind (Romans 12:2); and instead of being bound by bitterness, you will be motivated to think differently by the knowledge that as a man thinks in his heart, so is he (Proverbs 23:7, KJV).

BEAUTY FOR ASHES

The Lord wants to set you free. The route to freedom begins a personal relationship with Him (see Appendix). You can be free from the shackles of envy. You can be released from the burden of discouragement. He lifts the weight of bitterness. God will replace the ashes of your hurt with beauty; He wants to lift the spirit of heaviness and give you, instead, a garment of praise (Isaiah 61:3). God did all of this for my husband and me, and He will do it in your life, too (Acts 10:34). It is our desire that you meet the Father of Mercies and the God of all Comfort. It is He who comforts and heals us in all our troubles. Therefore, we write with the mission of 2 Corinthians 1:3–4 (NKJV):

> Blessed be the God and Father of our Lord Jesus Christ, the Father of mercies and God of all comfort, who comforts us in all our tribulation, that we may be able to comfort those who are in any trouble, with the [same] comfort with which we ourselves are comforted by God.

In His Service,
Jerome and Valerie

SECTION ONE
ENVY

CHAPTER

1

THE STING
OF ENVY

A sound heart is the life of the flesh:
but envy the rottenness of the bones.
—PROVERBS 14:30 KJV

It used to be a poison within me: a toxin that killed my hopes, contaminated my relationships, and polluted my thoughts. Envy was a thorn that had pierced my heart and tainted everything I believed, felt, and reasoned.

I was obsessed; I constantly compared myself to others. The cycle started with frustration and self-pity. Then something would happen to awaken the envy—usually it was some wonderful thing that happened to someone else. Their blessing grieved me. "Why them and not me?" I wondered. Of course, this type of thinking led to speculation. I dissected them and myself—always asking, "What is wrong with me and what is so darn 'right' with them?" I looked at others with suspicion. I studied their character, personality, and appearance. I inevitably found a flaw in them which always led me to the same conclusion: Life was just not fair.

Envy chewed away at my gut. With no cure in sight, I became critical and mean-spirited—totally self-absorbed. Not only did envy consume me; it gnawed at my friendships. But most importantly, it eroded my relationship with God. I just could not see my blessings. Why should I thank God when my desires were unfulfilled? I felt neglected by Him and I was miserable. I was ashamed of my pettiness and wallowed in self-pity. I never talked about how I felt. I kept my ugly little secret to myself.

FELICIA

The first person I clearly remember envying was my girlfriend Felicia. We met on an ordinary Sunday. Church was crowded, as usual, and I squeezed into the mid-row seat next to her just before the service started. Felicia pulled out a pen and a well-worn notebook filled with neatly printed notes; and just as if she were taking a class, she flipped to a blank page and systematically dated it. Being new to the church scene, I had never seen anyone who wanted to take notes during a service.

My curiosity piqued. I turned and said, "Hi, my name is Valerie. Why do you need a notebook in church?" Felicia graciously explained that she took notes of the sermon and, much to my amazement, she showed me notes she had taken two and three years prior. Felicia then introduced me to her fiancé, Sterling, who was seated on the other side of her. By the time the service was finished, she and I had exchanged telephone numbers.

Over the next few months, Felicia and I became very close friends. We enjoyed each other's company and knew some of the same people. We were both Deltas and "heavyweight champions" when it came to shopping and talking. We chatted about everything, including her upcoming marriage to Sterling and who I was currently dating. But above all of that good-girlfriend kind of stuff, the thing Felicia and I did best together was laugh. She was the kind of friend you could look at and sense what she was thinking—which always led to a good old-fashioned belly laugh.

Felicia and Sterling were married on a bright summer afternoon. She had it all: a terrific man, the wedding of her dreams, a ton of gifts, and not one, but two honeymoons. However, Felicia didn't just disappear; she remained my friend even after she got married. Overall, I thought Felicia's life overflowed with excitement, beauty, and love, while my days felt gray, monotonous, and boring. I was restlessly waiting for love. I saw myself as a jogger on the dating treadmill—and it didn't look like I was getting off any time soon. I just wanted one special someone to call my own.

Before their first wedding anniversary, Sterling and Felicia moved into an attractive three-story townhouse on a peaceful tree-lined street complete with a loft, a deck, and a hammock. I remained single—my sister and I lived together.

By their second anniversary, Sterling surprised Felicia with a new candy-apple red convertible topped with a satiny white gift bow. It was when Felicia roared into my driveway with her new car that I clearly remember feeling the sharp stab of envy. My life held few surprises. My singleness persisted, my sister was still my roommate, and I continued to drive my orange Corolla with the beige vinyl top.

By their third anniversary, Sterling and Felicia moved to a beautiful home nestled in an upscale area of the hills. I, however, was still very single, living with my sister, chugging along in my old orange car, and I was envious.

Around their fourth wedding anniversary, Felicia announced that she wanted to get pregnant, and she did so almost immediately. She also proclaimed that she wanted the baby to be born on Christmas Day. She was *not due* on Christmas Day; the baby was due in mid-January. Felicia had the baby on Christmas Day.

I was too through!!! Everything Felicia ever wanted, she always got—and quickly. The things I desired, I never seemed to get. Life looked so easy for her, yet it was hard for me. Life achievements happened quickly for Felicia. But in comparison, I had to work hard for whatever I got, and it came very slowly. I began to wonder what was wrong with me and, on the flip side, what was right with her. I wanted to marry and share my life with that special man. I desired to have a nice home, a family, and I sure could have used a new car. I, too, wanted the wonderful gifts life had to offer. *I envied Felicia—I just couldn't help it!*

YOUR ENVY LEVEL

Everyone experiences envy at one time or another. If you're anything like me, you too feel as though you "just can't help it." When you look around, weighing the chances of your dreams coming true, things look bleak. What you thought you would have achieved by now—hasn't happened. Where you thought you would be—you're nowhere near it. The person whom you thought you would be with—doesn't even know you exist. And time keeps marching by, relentlessly reminding you that you're not getting any younger and your precious dreams have not yet come true. On the other hand, there's someone in your life who seems to have it all. Or, if they don't, what they do have looks pretty darn good. Are you envious? Just take this little test and see.

QUIZ: HAVE YOU BEEN STUNG BY ENVY?

Instructions: Take this easy quiz by writing down the point value of the answer that best describes how you think or feel **most of the time** about the following situations. ("Never" is equal to 1 point and "Always" equals 7 points.)

1 Never   2 Very Seldom   3 Seldom   4 Sometimes
5 Often   6 Very Often   7 Always

1. I am unhappy about some aspect of my life (e.g., my career, where I live, my childhood, my love life, my parents, my looks, my level of education, my car, my weight, my finances).

2. I am "behind schedule." I feel bad about where I am in life.

3. God seems to be ignoring my prayers.

4. I don't feel valued because there is no special man who loves me.

5. I can't seem to help it, but I compare my life and situation to someone else.

6. When someone shares good news with me, I feel pain instead of happiness for them.

7. I feel shame when asked "Why aren't you married?"

8. I am angry that my desires are unfulfilled.

9. I am critical of myself.

10. I feel my dreams, goals, and desires are elusive (seem to be outside of my grasp).

Scoring: *Add the point values for each of your responses to get "Your Envy Level" score.*

10–30 Points
In this season of your life, envy is not a major problem. You are satisfied with yourself and your achievements. However,

seasons change. As surely as summer turns to autumn and later slides into winter—sooner or later, envy comes. Therefore, it is wise to equip yourself now.

31–50 Points

You experience envy every so often, and this is absolutely normal. There are areas of your life that you desire to be different, but they're not . . . yet. In fact, you probably have a difficult time recognizing the times you feel envious. You just know that you don't feel too good about a situation. These thoughts seem to come out of nowhere, and they take you by surprise. You will learn how to recognize envy and take control of those thoughts.

51–70 Points

You suffer with envy. You constantly compare yourself with others, observing them closely, measuring their lives, wondering why they seem to be blessed but not you. You are dealing with the very issues we are addressing. Living like this hurts. Not only is your self-esteem injured, but your interpersonal relationships are hampered. You can have the victory over envy, if you are willing to put forth the effort.

Let's take a closer look at envy.

2

EXPOSING
ENVY

*You cannot depend on your eyes
when your imagination is out of focus.*
—MARK TWAIN

THE YOUNG ATHLETE

Envy is best described by this ancient legend:

There was once a young athlete who competed wholeheartedly in the public games and lost. The people of the town erected a great statue to honor the winner. Filled with envy, the despondent loser decided he would destroy the statue. Every night, after it was dark, he would chisel at the base of the statue to weaken its foundation. Finally, the disgruntled young athlete succeeded and the sculpture toppled; but it fell on him and he died—a victim of his own envy.[1]

Envy is torture. It gnaws away at you, grates on your mind, and corrodes your self-esteem. Just like the young athlete, we, too, can become despondent. In our own hearts, under the cover of darkness, we chip away at those we envy. Envy separates us from friends and loved ones because envy is the nasty secret we keep to ourselves.

I never verbalized to anyone that I was envious. It was too ugly to share. This secret became the horrible part of myself I didn't want others to know about. Even before that, I didn't realize that envy was what I was feeling. Why? Because I didn't know what envy looked like. For me, "envy" was just a word—not a feeling. However, once I learned how to recognize envy and admit that I was envious, half the battle was won. The first step to victory over envy is to learn how to recognize it. Let's take a look at envy and expose envy's inky darkness to the illuminating light of our awareness.

WHAT IS ENVY?

According to the *Random House College Dictionary*, envy is:

a sense of discontent . . . with regard to another's advantages, success or possessions, etc. Desire for an advantage possessed by another. Ill will.

Envy has been described as "the unpleasant feeling of wanting what another person has and feeling bad that you don't have it."[2] There is a well-known emotional component to envy—it is pain. Envy produces emotional pain. When envy is fully entrenched in our lives, we can actually feel the physical sensation of pain at hearing another's good news. This is why envy has also been defined as "sorrow for the neighbor's good . . . (or) sorrow over one's own lack of good."[3] Envy produces dejection.

The word *envy* comes from the Latin word *invida* and French word *invidere* meaning to look askance at, or to see.[4]

In Romans 1:29 (NKJV), God includes envy in a list of actions that deserve death:

. . . *being filled with all unrighteousness, sexual immorality, wickedness, covetousness, maliciousness,* **full of envy,** *murder, strife, deceit, evil-mindedness* . . . (emphasis added)

God also warns us about envy in Proverbs 3:31; Proverbs 14:30; Proverbs 23:17; Philippians 1:15; 1 Timothy 6:4; and James 3:14, 16. Jesus was crucified because He was envied (Matthew 27:18; Mark 15:10); Joseph was sold into slavery because his brothers envied him (Acts 7:9 KJV); Abraham was envied for his possessions (Genesis 26:14); Paul and Barnabas were kicked out of town because of envy (Acts 13:45 KJV); and a riotous crowd broke into Jason's house in search of Paul and Silas and dragged Jason through the city because of envy (Acts 17:5–9 KJV). Many times, envy is at the root of many actions, such as theft, gossip, revenge, libel, kidnapping, civil unrest, vandalism, lawsuits, shoplifting, malice, bragging, covetousness, resentment, contempt, and even murder.

What is it about envy that makes it so deadly? The author of *The Tyranny of Malice*, Joseph Berke, sums it up the best:

> Envy is a state of exquisite tension, torment and ill will provoked by an overwhelming sense of inferiority, importance and worthlessness. It begins in the eye of the beholder and is so painful to the mind, that the envious person will go to almost any lengths to diminish, if not destroy whatever, or whoever may have aroused it.[5]

WHAT DO WE ENVY?

Envy is a sin that comes from comparing yourself with another person. Well-known theorist of social behavior Helmut Schoeck stated that "envy is a drive which lies at the core of man's life as a social being, and which occurs as soon as two individuals become capable of mutual comparison."[6]

We can envy anything that we consider valuable, whether it is a personality trait, a physical attribute, social status, or possession. For example:

- Angela, now forty pounds overweight, resents her girlfriend Lynn's shapely figure.
- Laura feels overlooked, and she envies her coworker Julie's promotion.
- Monica, divorced mother of two boys, envies her cousin Kathy's free time because she doesn't have children.

- Leslie envies her mother because she was born in a time when it was "easier" to get married and men were willing to make a commitment.
- Yolanda, a size "A" cup, longs for "D"-sized breasts like Carmen.
- Tiffany hates pressing her hair; she envies her girlfriend Danielle's naturally wavy hair.
- Kimberlee feels ignored and undesirable; she wants men to look at her the same way they look at her older sister Dawn.
- Melanie dislikes her deep chocolate skin tone and wishes her skin was the same bronze coloring as her play-cousin Christina.
- Eve envied Gwen from the time they were children because Gwen was raised in a home where both parents were present and loved her.
- Lillian would give anything to have had the opportunity to go to college like her younger sister Barbara.

It is especially easy to envy a trait in someone when we feel deficient or lacking in a particular area.

WHAT IS THE DIFFERENCE BETWEEN ENVY AND JEALOUSY?

As we have seen, envy is the sin of comparing ourselves with another and desiring what they have. Jealousy is similar to envy in that we have a rival with whom we are competing. However, jealousy always revolves around a third person.

Jealousy is the hurtful feeling involved in competing with someone else for the affection of another. Jealousy also encompasses suspicion and a heightened sense of awareness about the actions and whereabouts of the loved one. For example, Janet, Mariah, and Steven all attend the same church. Janet and Steven are dating, but their relationship is still pretty new. Janet is jealous of Mariah because she and Steven always seem to have great conversations and they laugh a lot together. Because Janet is serious by nature, she and Steven rarely joke with each other. Steven has no idea that his conversations with Mariah are making Janet uncomfortable. However, whenever Janet sees Steven with Mariah she feels jealousy. Mariah, on the other hand, is envious of Janet because she drives a car Mariah would love to own. As for her feelings about Steven, he reminds Mariah of her little brother.

STRATEGIC MOVES

1. What do you dislike about yourself?

2. What attribute does someone have that you wished you possessed?

In summary, we have discussed that envy is "the unpleasant feeling of wanting what another person has and feeling bad you don't have it." We have discovered that envy produces emotional pain and that God says that envy is sin. We have also learned that we can envy anything—a physical attribute, a personal possession, or a marital state. We have uncovered that envy and jealousy are different. But how can we recognize envy? Are there symptoms or telltale signs to help us identify when we are feeling envious?

3

ENVY'S
HIDDEN
SYMPTOMS

*If we claim to be without sin, we deceive ourselves
and the truth is not in us.*
—I JOHN 1:8

Envy is not like lightning. Lightning is sudden, abrupt, and un-predictable—it disappears as quickly as it comes. Envy does not oc-cur suddenly, although we may feel as if we've been suddenly struck by envy. Nor is it abrupt, even though we are often startled by its unexpected appearance. And envy certainly doesn't disappear quick-ly. In fact, it continues to linger and as a result our mind dwells on the object of envy long after it has left the scene.

Although envy seems to appear out of thin air—it doesn't. It's like that magician's trick of pulling a rabbit out of a hat. The illusion is: The hat is empty, yet a bunny mysteriously emerges. However, the bunny doesn't just appear. The truth is: The rabbit was already hid-den in the hat. The presence of envy is just like that old magician's trick—envy, like the rabbit, is already present; it is just hidden inside.

We are born with envy. It is present in the heart of every human being and is part of our sin nature. Fortunately for us, a great deal of the time, envy is "asleep." For some of us, envy slumbers for years before it's awakened. For others, envy only seems to doze, because every time they turn around they're dealing with envy. So the question then becomes, what awakens envy?

The emotion that arouses envy is one that we call *"intense desire."* Of course, we all have desires, but not all desires stir up envy. Some desires are fleeting, passing fancies—those that come and go depending upon our moods. Other desires are like pleasant dreams; they are "nice to have" but you know that you could live your life very well without them. The desire that stirs up envy is different. The object of this desire is perceived to improve the quality of one's life. We long for the desired object, we think about it, and we imagine what our lives would be like with this desire fulfilled. This desire is special because it meets an emotional, mental, or physical need.

In the previous chapter, we have seen that the desire can be for anything from a physical attribute to a talent or possession. An intense desire can be recognized because no matter how deeply the desire is buried, it can cause envy to suddenly surface when you unexpectedly walk into a situation. But envy is not the only emotion felt in circumstances like that. There are other feelings that generally accompany envy.

Envy seldom travels alone. In fact, envy has "symptoms" just like the flu has its own set of symptoms. These indicators reveal (1) our susceptibility to envy or (2) the activity of envy already in our life. The symptoms are frustration, self-pity, grasping, and begrudging questioning.

FRUSTRATION

We have all been frustrated at one time or another. It's the feeling that follows when we try to accomplish a goal, achieve a dream, or attempt something new, only to have our efforts amount to nothing. Imagine trying to paddle a canoe upstream against the current and no matter how much effort you expend, no forward progress is made. Frustration is disappointment mixed with anger, accompanied by the feelings of hopelessness and confusion. Important features of frustration are puzzlement, wonder, and not knowing what to do to change the outcome. The emotion embodies the idea that obstacles greater than yourself are blocking the goal and, regardless of what you do, the goal is elusive and only the obstacles remain.

Many unmarried women feel a great deal of frustration when they desire to become married and they are not. Their frustration can result after years of dating or years of not even being asked out on a date; of being told they were too shy or too intimidating; not being beautiful enough or being "too beautiful"; being full-figured or being too flat; or being too light or too dark. Regardless of the obstacle—it's always something. The bottom line is that the frustration remains, while the goal, dream, or achievement seems out of reach and all the obstacles are still there.

SELF-PITY

Self-pity is the second symptom of envy. Self-pity is the "poor me" attitude that causes us to mope and whine about our situation. The dangerous element of self-pity is that it promotes the belief that we are helpless and our situation is hopeless. The sense of helplessness and hopelessness comes from looking back at our unsuccessful attempts and, as a result, sorrow sets in. Self-pity causes us to dwell on everything that is wrong in our lives. We throw up our hands and declare we can no longer fight for our goal. We're miserable, and we have reached a point where we believe we've endured frustration long enough. A part of us has already given up, and we feel sorry for ourselves because we believe that the dream may not be possible or the goal is unobtainable.

Self-pity is dangerous because it causes us to focus only on what is wrong or missing in our lives. It narrows our vision so that we only see that which has caused us frustration. We tend to ignore the amazing and wonderful aspects of our lives. We lose the ability to be grateful for what we do have. We desire only that which appears to be out of reach, and as a result, we feel sorry for ourselves and discouraged about our situation.

Advanced stages of self-pity lead to an apathy about life. We feel a loss of interest, a gray dullness sets in, hope fades away, and we feel listless. Feeling hopeless and paralyzed in one area of life often spreads to other areas as well. Gloom and self-pity because of the lack of a romantic relationship can easily affect our work and church life, or other areas. Self-pity signals that hope of obtaining the dream is dying.

GRASPING

Grasping occurs when we will do *anything* to obtain the desired goal while ignoring the consequences. We're willing to compromise our values, our beliefs, and everything we may have stood for in the past in order to obtain our desire.

Grasping is best portrayed by a gambler who believes he has a winning hand in a high-stakes poker game and it's his turn to "ante up" or "fold." He's willing to wager *all* his money *and* his house because he believes he can win the jackpot.[1] Women do the same thing. In the hopes that we will make a man love us, we gamble with everything we have. We think we have a "good hand": we're attractive, employed, a nice person, and, in addition to that, it's time to get married! The "jackpot": He looks like he is exactly what we want and need. He's the best thing that's come into our lives in a long time. We "ante up" to stay in the game: We overlook the point that he hasn't made a commitment, we ignore the fact that he's critical, and although we may have been celibate, we compromise and have sex because we don't want to lose him. That's what grasping is: It's the willingness to ignore the pitfalls and compromise in the hope of obtaining what we want.

BEGRUDGING QUESTIONING

Another symptom of envy is "begrudging questioning." We have all wondered how a particular woman has ended up with an incredibly handsome man. We wonder, "What on earth does he see in her?" That is an example of begrudging questioning. It is the thinly veiled resentment of envious people wondering why another has what they want and murmuring about the unfairness of it all. To begrudge involves the belief that an injustice has occurred, and therefore it is painful to see the other's blessing.

Begrudging questioning actually goes much further than mere annoyance or irritation. We question the "fairness" of God. "Why did He answer *her* prayer for a husband, and not *mine*? She's only twenty-five, and I'm forty-two—she's got time, I don't. It's just not fair!" We feel that God *owes* us the answer to our prayer. Begrudging questioning is the continued muttering and murmuring that comes from our sense of entitlement—that something due to us is being withheld.

STRATEGIC MOVES

1. What are you frustrated about?

2. What obstacles are keeping you from your goal?

3. Which of these symptoms have you seen in your own life?

Remember, we've learned that envy doesn't just appear, but it has always been present inside us. Envy is a part of our sin nature. No one is free from envy; all of us experience it at one time or another in our life. We've also discovered that envy is aroused as a result of an unfulfilled intense desire. We have uncovered that envy isn't a stand-alone emotion, but it is usually accompanied by telltale symptoms like frustration, self-pity, grasping, and begrudging questioning. We have all experienced these feelings, but what if we are behind schedule? Suppose we feel envy because we've been waiting for something that has never come into our lives?

CHAPTER

4

I'M BEHIND SCHEDULE: ENVY AS A RESULT OF UNFULFILLED DREAMS

Hope deferred makes the heart sick ...
—PROVERBS 13:12

Ja'Nette is a forty-four-year-old prosecuting attorney who has worked for the D.A.'s office for the last sixteen years. She has a great deal going for herself, but none of that matters because she's "behind schedule." Long hours and a heavy caseload featuring a wide array of Black men entangled in the web of the justice system have convinced Ja'Nette that there are no good Black men left. Ja'Nette has her own home, drives a late-model car, and is quite beautiful, but none of that matters because she's lonely.

Ja'Nette thought she would have been married by now. Thinking about her age and her single state makes her feel resentful. After all, she's in her mid-forties, has never married, and still doesn't know how to answer that painful and frequently asked question, "Why haven't you gotten married?" Ja'Nette is envious of women who are married. She can't seem to figure out how they ended up with a husband and why she is alone. After all, many of the married women she knows don't look half as good as she does, nor are they as smart.

Ja'Nette hurts the most at church, particularly if she is sitting next to or behind an affectionate couple. The place that should give her hope only seems to make her loneliness more pronounced. As of last year, she stopped going to weddings and has sworn off all bridal or baby showers. She has found that it just takes too long for her to recover emotionally. Ja'Nette can't share her feelings with her married friends because they just don't understand. No one ever talks about envy, so she just stuffs her feelings down inside and continues with her life.

OUR EXPECTATIONS

Dreams of a beautiful white gown, rows of smiling friends, a handsome groom, an exchange of rings, and the toss of a bouquet—these images have been with us since childhood. We *expected* to meet our soul mate—the one we would spend the rest of our lives with. It never occurred to us that we would be single. If, in our teens, we were asked would we be married, unhesitatingly we would have answered, "Yes." Even in our twenties, we thought, "No problem!" By the time we hit our thirties, we start to wonder; and by our forties, we are fighting panic. Some of us have the added dimension of being a single parent. We may have been divorced or widowed or we mistakenly thought we met the man of our dreams—only to be left raising his child(ren) on our own. The bottom line is: Where we are, we did not *expect* to be.

Instead of being married and fulfilling what we thought was a logical step in our life plan, we're trying to hustle up an escort to the office Christmas party and dodging questions about our dating lives from well-meaning family members.

LEFT BEHIND

There are times we can't help feeling left behind by girlfriends who marry. They expect us to come to their baby showers and cheer them on as their lives progress, while we feel stuck in the same place. Although we are happy for our friends, sometimes we have to beat back feelings of envy and anger. We may even feel out of step with the rest of society. No matter how accomplished we have become in other areas of our life, without that special someone, we still feel fearful, incomplete, and like a failure. Everyone and everything around us seems to shout that we are alone. It is in this environment that we begin to examine those around us who have married. What is it about them that attracted their mates to them? We drill our friends with questions trying to discover what makes them different from us. We're trying to discover the secret. We're looking for the "key" that has opened the door of marriage to them because perhaps that same key will work for us.

We examine our girlfriends because we are envious. We scrutinize them with the same intensity we would use to inspect an insect under a magnifying glass. We look at their appearance: how they wear their hair, their skin tone, their sense of style, and their figure. Perhaps the key is in the clothes they wear, the car they drive, or the location or appearance of their home or apartment. We observe their personality: how they laugh and interact with others. Whatever it is that we determine to be the key many times reveals what we specifically envy about them.

There is an old adage that says, "Imitation is the sincerest flattery." To a degree that is true, but there is also a flip side to that statement. Imitation of someone else spotlights our inability to embrace ourselves for who we are. Whatever we have determined to be the key to our friend's success, we may try to imitate. We go into debt buying clothes, shoes, cars, and redecorating. By doing so, we slowly dismantle ourselves and become replicas of others. There is absolutely nothing wrong with self-improvement. However, the question becomes, Are we improving ourselves or trying to transform into someone else?

STRATEGIC MOVES

1. Where did you expect to be in life at this age?

2. Whose life have you examined?

3. What did you conclude?

IT'S NOT FAIR

Some of us are not imitators at all—that's not our issue. For example, during the process of examining our friend, suppose we conclude that our friend is *not* superior to us in any category, and we may actually deduce that she is subpar or deficient in some area compared to us. She may not be particularly pretty, witty, or personable. In fact, a lot of people just don't like her. So what is it about her that causes her to be blessed? That kind of question gnaws at us; it rumbles around in the back of our minds; it colors how we see her. We now see her flaws—we scrutinize what is wrong with her. The closer we look at her, the more we're convinced that life is just not fair. There is a feeling of randomness, that things just occur without reason. If there was reason—of course, we would have been married by now.

This *begrudging questioning* thought pattern of "why her and not me?" is cyclical in nature because it does not lead to a forthcoming answer. This kind of question is like a fish bone stuck in our throats; it's an irritant. The "why her and not me?" question escorts us to *frustration* because there is no forthcoming answer. Then we're propelled on to *self-pity* because we begin to believe that we are the victim of an injustice.

Whenever we ask why someone is blessed, the question stems from a root of envy. Whether we ask because we believe the other person to be "inferior" to us in some way or because we can clearly see that they are superior to us—it is merely evidence of two sides of the same coin: envy. The reality is that our assessment of superiority or inferiority comes from whatever our own particular mind-set— it certainly is not from the mind of God.

God uniquely created each of us to have relationship with Him (see Appendix). We were never meant to be superior or inferior to each other; instead God has planned for us all (with our strengths, gifts, and failings) to be co-laborers together to accomplish His will here on earth. But we will never labor together when we see each other through the lens of envy, harbor self-pity, and wonder if we're "behind schedule."

GOD, WHERE ARE YOU?

Where is God when we are battling the fact that the years are ticking by and we're not where we thought we would be? The life of a single woman is not at all what the TV commercials advertise. "How long is this going to go on?" we wonder as we watch our friends with their husbands beside them, their houses filled with wonderful wedding gifts, and their cute little babies who have larger wardrobes than we have.

"Where is God in all of this?" "Doesn't He see what is happening here?" "Why hasn't He answered my prayer for a husband yet?" "What is taking so long?" "Doesn't He see that I am embarrassed every time people ask if I'm married?" "Doesn't He care that I'm in pain?" These are questions that we ask God and ask others about God when we are in pain. Most people don't know what to say. Our questions seem to dangle in midair with no one to catch them. Our family and friends just nod their heads, pat us on the shoulder, and give us meaningless platitudes like, "It will all work out." But it hasn't worked out in the past, and it's not working out now. "Where is God? Is God ignoring me?"

5

FREE YOURSELF FROM TRAPPED THINKING: GOD IS IGNORING ME

I call on you, O God, for you will answer me;
give ear to me and hear my prayer.
—PSALM 17:6

One of the most painful experiences in life is to be ignored by the ones whom you care for and love. A fundamental human desire is to be acknowledged and have our needs met. For example, when one sibling feels ignored by a parent or is not getting the same amount of time and attention as another, the results can cause hurt and division. In addition, the pain of being ignored by those around us is magnified depending on how close we are to them. Therefore, to be ignored can be a traumatic experience.

Nevertheless, there is nothing more painful than to think that we are being intentionally forgotten by God, our heavenly Father. This is true because the deepest level of intimacy that we can experience in this life is our spiritual connection and relationship with God. There are many things in life that we can allow to break this spiritual bond—and envy is one of them. When this intimate bond is broken, we feel abandoned and alone in the world. In our aloneness, we conclude that God must be ignoring us.

Whenever envy controls our lives, our relationship with God and our view of Him suffers greatly. This is true because we often blame God for not giving us what we desire. As a result, we believe He is ignoring us. When we think God is ignoring us, we say things like:

- "He is neglecting me."
- "Where is God in my life?"
- "He doesn't love me because He hasn't answered my prayer."
- "Others are more important to Him."
- "He's never around when I need Him."

If you have consuming thoughts like these, you are suffering from trapped thinking. These types of thoughts separate us from God. There is no deeper hurt than when we mistakenly believe that the God who loves and adores us has turned His back on us. And guess what? Satan loves it when we believe that God is ignoring us—he wouldn't have it any other way. Satan wants us to believe that we are "behind schedule" and will never catch up. It is his job to steal, kill, and destroy (John 10:10a) the truth of how God really feels about us. Satan wants to kill our faith and destroy our relationship with God. He uses envy to confuse us (James 3:16 KJV) while leading us to think something other than the truth that God loves us, cares for us, and has our best interest at heart.

God comes to us to give life and to build loving relationships (John 10:10b; 13:34–35). Satan comes to break relationships by pitting us against God and others. When we believe that God is ignoring us, we are actually giving in to the lie that says, "God refuses to take notice of me." We are believing that God has shut His eyes to our needs or is willfully disregarding us. Ultimately, it is an untruth that causes us to believe God has overlooked or rejected us. Envy truly does inspire wrong thinking about God.

NEVER FORGOTTEN

There is never a moment when God is not aware of where we are and where He is taking us. In other words, He does not forget us, and He is always working things out for our best. This may be hard to believe in the midst of our frustration, but it's true. The emotions produced by years of unanswered prayers (frustration), unfulfilled dreams (despair), and blocked goals (failure) are very real. To free yourself from the belief that God is ignoring you and eliminate the bondage that those feelings are sure to produce, you must replace them with three truths that must be permanently deposited in your heart:

- Truth #1: God Has a Plan for Your Life
- Truth #2: He Will Never Leave You Nor Forsake You
- Truth #3: God Causes All Things to Work Out for Your Good

Let's take a closer look at these three important truths.

TRUTH #1: GOD HAS A PLAN FOR YOUR LIFE

Did you know that God has a specific, detailed plan for your life? Whenever you feel that He has left you behind without any hope or future, He wants to remind you not to believe it. God knows that there will be times when we will not understand or see His plan for us. As a result, He reassures us with these words:

"I know the plans I have for you," declares the LORD, "plans to prosper you and not to harm you, plans to give you hope and a future."
(Jeremiah 29:11)

Whenever you feel yourself slipping back into believing that you are being ignored by God, you must learn how to "KNOW."

K—Keep: *God will keep His promises.* Since He promises that He knows the plan that He has for your life, take Him at His Word and believe it!

N—Now: *No one plans their future without planting seeds now.* Remember God is working on your future right now, no matter how your current circumstances may look.

O—Opportunity: *Since God helps you live His plan each day, take advantage of every opportunity.* Redeem the time by acknowledging God and doing good.

W—Worship: *Worship God in advance for the hope you have in your God-directed future.* Say good things about Him. Worship will give God glory and encourage your heart.

Ultimately, you must trust in the God who knows the plan that He has for you.

TRUTH #2: HE WILL NEVER LEAVE YOU NOR FORSAKE YOU

One sunny June afternoon, a father, James, took his son, Justin, to the park. It was Justin's favorite park because it was large with endless opportunities for running, jumping, swinging, and sliding. It was an obstacle course of pure fun. James loved the park because no matter what bench he sat on, he could see Justin's every move without obstruction. Justin felt comfortable going from the jungle gyms to the slides to the swings all by himself because he knew his father was always watching him. Justin played anywhere in the park and never felt alone. The only reason Justin had the confidence to run freely around the park is because he had no doubt that his father was watching him.

This is a great example of a father who never lets his son out of his sight. It's also indicative of how God never lets us out of His sight. God promises you that He will never leave you nor forsake you (Hebrews 13:5). No matter where you are, what you feel, or what you're going through, this promise is true. God is always there for you.

You may ask:

- "Where is God in all this?" He says, "I will never leave you nor forsake you."
- "Why hasn't He answered my prayer for a husband?" He says, "I will never leave you nor forsake you."
- "What's taking so long?" He says, "I will never leave you nor forsake you."
- "Doesn't He care that I'm in pain?" He says, "I will never leave you nor forsake you."

God does not answer all our questions in the time that we desire, but we can be assured that He is with us. Knowing God is watching your every move will give you the same comfort and security little Justin has with his father.

TRUTH #3: GOD CAUSES ALL THINGS TO WORK OUT FOR YOUR GOOD

This third truth takes a lot of courage and a relentless attitude to apply. If you do what it takes, your life will be changed forever. You will experience the love of God and a freedom for living as never before. Here is the victory that God gives you in all of your circumstances:

And we know that in all things God works for the good of those who love him, who have been called according to his purpose.
(Romans 8:28)

This is a powerful promise. At first glance, it may seem that this verse is saying that everything that happens to us is good. We know that is not true. But He *is* saying that in everything that happens, He will work it into something good if we love Him and let Him. In other words, instead of ignoring you, God is adoring you by working your situation out for your good and His glory. Once a day, for the next thirty days, read aloud the following affirmation based on Romans 8:28 and let it change your perspective on life forever.

And We Know—I know that God's Word is true for me. I will not doubt His promises toward me. I will trust His words, no matter what my circumstances may be. I will "know."

In All Things God Works for the Good—Today I choose to believe that God is working every detail of my life out for my good. He will take all my problems and create something helpful out of them. I refuse to believe that He is not working in my best interest at all times.

Of Those Who Love Him—God is working things out for me because I love Him. Not because I am doing all the right things. I will continue to show my love for Him by trusting Him with every circumstance in my life.

Who Have Been Called According to His Purpose—God is on my side because I am His child. I am His child because I have accepted Christ into my heart. As His child, He will not fail to carry out His purpose for my life. I have been called according to His purpose, not my own.

By believing and applying these three truths in your life, you will know that God is not ignoring you.

STRATEGY FOR PEACE

Take time now to pray. You can use the sample prayer included below or pray a similar prayer of your own.

Heavenly Father:

I have learned that You have a plan for my life because You want me to have hope and a future (Jeremiah 29:11). I need hope in my future because I have been carrying the burden of envy. I now realize that You consider envy to be a sin. I desire to have victory over envy. I am now aware of what envy is and will be alert to its symptoms. With Your help, I take a stand against envy in my life.

Also, I have believed that You were ignoring me. I now know that is not true. The Bible says in Hebrews 13:5 that You will never leave me nor will You abandon or forsake me. By faith, I have made up my mind to believe Your promise. Please help me to know You as my ever-present help (Psalm 46:1). I choose to escape from this type of trapped thinking.

In the name of Jesus.
Amen.

6

SUCCEED NOW: CONQUER FEELING LIKE A FAILURE

*... in all these things we are more
than conquerors through him who loved us.*
—ROMANS 8:37

The feeling of envy that results from believing we are "behind schedule" is supported by twin foundational beams: (1) our trapped thinking that God is ignoring us and (2) our sense of failure. To dismantle this kind of envy in our lives, it is critical to use a dual-pronged attack. In chapter 5, we addressed and acted to counter the faulty thinking that God is ignoring us. Now we are going to target our feeling like a failure. To attack envy that stems from a sense of failure, take the following steps:

DON'T ISOLATE YOURSELF

True victory over envy cannot be achieved by simply making up your mind not to be envious anymore. But we can have victory through connection—by having a healthy relationship with God and healthy connections with others. Our most important relationship, however, is with God. *It is only the power of God that can truly set us free* from envy and other emotional afflictions like bitterness, unforgiveness, discouragement, and anger. Without a relationship with God, there is always that longing that we try to fill by pursuing relationships with men, submerging ourselves into our careers, buying new clothes, and rushing around here and there just keeping ourselves too busy to think. Those are all temporary solutions to a spiritual problem that has eternal consequences. When these temporary solutions don't work, we may try to dull the longing/pain with people-pleasing, perfectionism, sex, alcohol, having a know-it-all attitude, drugs, gambling, and the like. In order to have true victory over your emotions, you need a real anchor—and that anchor is God.

In order to establish your connection with God, you must have a relationship with His Son Jesus. Only Jesus is the solution to that longing. Take action right now to establish a relationship with Jesus, Son of God. He came to earth with the primary mission of bringing mankind back to God (John 6:35–40). Jesus manifested the power of God here on earth during His time of ministry. Then, at the appointed time, He laid down His life as a sacrifice for the sins of mankind (Romans 5:6–10; Hebrews 9:28). Jesus died, He was buried, and on the third day He was resurrected by God (Acts 2:22–24, 31–33). He was seen by over five hundred people (1 Corinthians 15:3–6). Later Jesus ascended into heaven (Luke 24:51) where He is seated at the right hand of God (Hebrews 8:1–2; 1 Peter 3:21–22), praying and interceding for us right now (Hebrews 7:25).

The question then becomes: Do you want God in your life or do you still want to live it without Him? It's easy to ask God into your life—it's just a whisper away by praying to God. See the Appendix if you want to surrender your life to God by accepting that Jesus died for your sins. By doing this, you then have a relationship with God. There are many benefits to having this relationship with God; one of them is that you can live with Him forever in heaven after you die. By never accepting the sacrifice of Jesus dying for you, you live your life without a relationship with God. Then when you die, you will forever be outside the presence of God. It's an important decision to make now—while you can. When you enter into relationship with God, you no longer have to wonder about your worth, your plans, or your purpose. From the time you accept Christ into your life, He begins revealing His plan for you as you get to know Him.

ACKNOWLEDGE YOUR FEELINGS

There is nothing like honesty. God invites you to share your feelings with Him. In fact, God longs for your honesty. Tell Him how you feel about being single. Explain to Him that you feel that you're behind schedule, that you have feelings of failure in that area of your life. Divulge whom you have been envious of and why. If you're angry with Him—say so. If you're disappointed, discouraged, irritated, embarrassed—get it out in the open. God can take it!

"Why?" you may ask. "If He's God of the universe, the Creator of the heavens and the earth, all-powerful and all-knowing, He already knows how I feel. Why do I have to share my feelings with Him?" Because it puts everything out on the table. Remember: your relationship with God is just that—a relationship. If you have a friend that you're irritated with, it is best not to ignore the situation and continue on in a strained relationship. Both you and your friend know that something is wrong. It is best to talk about it and get it out in the open. It's the same with God. By not talking about it, by stuffing your feelings in and not bringing them out into the open, your relationship with God remains strained and distant. Besides that, God is big enough to handle your anger or your sadness, whether you're moaning, crying, screaming, or mumbling—He understands, loves, and accepts you. The bottom line is that God welcomes us to come to Him and reason together with Him (Isaiah 1:18); and we have a standing invitation to do just that anytime, day or night.

Not only should we share our feelings with God; we should acknowledge our feelings to someone else also. God never intended for us to walk through life alone. As human beings, we were designed not only to have a relationship with Him, but to have meaningful relationships with one another. Part of having victory over envy is to bring envy out from under the covers—the secret parts of our hearts—and to tell someone that you are feeling envious. This person is not necessarily the person that you envy. Reach out and find someone who is experienced, perhaps an older woman. Talk about envy. Confess it. Choose carefully whom to share this with. Make sure that they will keep your confidence and not carelessly share your intimate feelings with others. Ask that person for support and encouragement as you take your stand against envy. Remember: the longer you keep the feeling of envy a secret, the stronger it grows. Part of defeating envy is to expose it and talk about it.

COMBAT FEAR

Fear plays a big role, not only in envy, but also in our sense of failure. When we feel that we are "behind schedule," we often let our imagination run wild and we become fearful about our future. Part of the feeling of failure comes with our mental projection that we'll remain in the same situation that we are in today. We think that because we may be experiencing loneliness today, in five or ten years from now we will still be lonely—only older. That is not true. Thoughts like these cause us to fear our future instead of embracing it. A wise person coined an acronym for the word "FEAR"—False Evidence Appearing Real.

One of my biggest fears was that I was not sure that marriage was God's will for my life. For many years, I was never certain of how God viewed my desire for marriage, and since I wasn't sure, my resolve would dissolve into wondering if God was in agreement with my prayer for a spouse. This fear was finally neutralized after I realized that the desire for marriage was given to me by God. I finally accepted that when you have an intimate relationship with God, it is He who puts His desires in us (Psalm 37:4), making His desires our desires.

The desire for marriage is a godly desire. It is God who created marriage (Genesis 2:24); it was He who said that it wasn't good for man to be alone; it was God who created Eve to be a helper for Adam (Genesis 2:18–22). Besides that, I knew I did not have the gift of singleness. I had to take the leap of faith and believe that it was God who gave me the desire for marriage and begin to trust that He would bring it to pass.

Feeling behind schedule is a manifestation of fear. The sensation of feeling behind happens at different ages for different people. Once the first sensation of feeling behind manifests itself, unless it is dealt with, the sensation continues to reoccur. My first sensation of feeling behind schedule was when I turned twenty-nine years old—because I realized I wouldn't meet my goal of getting married by thirty. For some women, the sensation of feeling behind begins in their early twenties. For others, it doesn't start until their late forties. For most of us, it occurs somewhere in between.

How do we conquer feeling behind schedule? By conquering our thoughts. Fear occurs because we paint different scenarios of failure on the screen of our imagination. We run little vignettes in our mind and let our imagination run wild. Whether we project ourselves into our own future and see misery, or we experience the sensation of being behind our self-invented schedule, the fear created is a work of our imagination. Regardless of what the imagined situation is, we are using our imagination to our detriment.

Our imagination is a very powerful God-given ability, and its use affects both our attitude and the direction of our life. God tells us what to do with these types imaginings. We are to take hold of (or take captive) these thoughts; we are not to let them prevail over what God says about us and our future (2 Corinthians 10:5). How do you do that? You must know what God says about you, and *you must repeat what He says*. Whenever the thought of being behind schedule comes into your mind, instead of entertaining it, tell the thought to go away and repeat what God says about you. If the thought comes back, you drive it away. Don't let these types of thoughts rob you of peace.

EMBRACE YOUR UNIQUENESS

Another important key for victory over envy as a result of feeling behind schedule is to "embrace your uniqueness." Discover who you are. Each of us is special and unique. It doesn't matter how much we may look, sound, or have tendencies like someone else—we are each wonderfully and individually made, down to our fingerprints and DNA (Psalm 139:14). Unfortunately, some of us have been told that we'll never amount to anything, we are no good, we're stupid, we're ugly, or any number of horrible and defeating things. Others of us have been told that we were unwanted as a baby, or we may have been conceived under unfortunate circumstances. In cases of deep emotional or psychological wounding, individual therapy with a Christian psychologist can go a long way to helping one embrace her uniqueness. But the ultimate bottom line is that God created us and wanted us on earth in this present time.

51

God created each of us with a specific purpose in mind, and He gave all of us the gifts we need to fulfill our destiny. The ultimate gift you can give yourself is to know your purpose and go about getting it accomplished. It wasn't until I took the time to discover my purpose, uncover my talents, and started moving toward my dream that my life took on new meaning. The step of embracing who you are takes time and energy because it requires us to be still and take account of ourselves. However, the lasting value of knowing your purpose and moving in that direction is wonderfully exciting and radically life-changing.

Lastly, a facet of embracing yourself is knowing that your worth is not given to you by a man. Having a man in your life doesn't suddenly give your life meaning. No! Your life has meaning now—just as you are. It is so sad to see women who do not see their value, attractiveness, talents, or self-worth because they have not had a boyfriend or husband confirm who they are. It is too often true that unless a man tells us we're beautiful, we don't accept our full lips, our well-rounded hips, our hair, our color, or our weight. Instead, embrace how you look. Accept what God says about you and learn to love yourself for who you are. When we accept, respect, and love ourselves, we become infinitely more attractive to others because our sense of worth radiates from within. We are complete and worthwhile individuals without a man in our life. Our value is confirmed by God—not by a man.

STRATEGY FOR PEACE

Below is a sample prayer. Fill in the blanks and find a quiet place and talk to God.

Heavenly Father:

I repent of envy because I now know that envy is sin. I have been envious of (fill in the blank with a name(s)) and this day I renounce being envious of them. I also confess to you my feelings of failure about (name what it is). I have also felt that I am behind schedule (I thought I would be "x" by this time); and I confess my frustrations about (fill in the blank).

Father, You created me for a specific purpose (Ephesians 1:11), and You gave me the gifts I need to fulfill that purpose (1 Peter 4:10). Please reveal to me the gifts that You have given me because it is against Your will that I be ignorant (1 Corinthians 12:1). Lord, help me to realize that my worth comes from You, and not from the presence or absence of a man in my life. Please reveal to me how You value and esteem me. One way You have already revealed Your love for me is that You sent Your Son Jesus to die for me (John 3:16).

Now Lord God, I ask You to give me peace. The Bible says that where there is envy and selfish ambition, we will find disorder (James 3:16). But You are the God of peace and not of disorder (1 Corinthians 14:33); therefore, I ask for You to give me peace. I thank You in advance for sending Your peace to me about my life and my circumstances. I know now that the peace of God surpasses my understanding, and it will guard my heart and my mind in Christ Jesus (Philippians 4:7). Thank You for hearing and answering my prayer.

7

I FEEL THREATENED: ENVY AS A RESULT OF RIVALRY

How depressing it can be
to witness the blessing of another.
—WILLIAM F. MAY[1]

TWO SISTERS

Monique and Jasmine are sisters who are fourteen months apart in age. From the time they could talk, they have argued, bickered, and fought with each other. Monique has always felt that Jasmine had it easy. Jasmine had asthma, and for a portion of her childhood she was confined to quiet activities. This enabled Jasmine to get out of a great deal of the housework, but it also meant Monique had to do more. Monique envied Jasmine because she didn't have to do all of the chores. The feeling that their parents favored Jasmine led Monique to compete with her sister for their attention.

The event that sealed Monique's resentment of Jasmine was when Jasmine was moved up from the fifth into the sixth grade with Monique. From that time forward, their competition intensified. In high school, Monique won several awards in track and field while Jasmine ran for and was elected student body president. Monique's envy seemed to grow in proportion to Jasmine's popularity. Although their parents equally expressed pride in both of their daughters, Monique thought she could detect more excitement about Jasmine's accomplishments.

Unintentionally, the sisters ended up at the same university, and of course, their competition continued. Monique majored in Psychology while Jasmine selected Computer Sciences. Much to Monique's irritation, Jasmine's grade point average was 3.65 compared to Monique's 3.4. By graduation, Jasmine had a job offer (which she accepted) from a well-known software designer in Washington which included a very generous salary, a moving allowance, and stock options. Monique didn't receive any job offers. After sending out over 100 résumés and going on several job interviews, Monique finally received a job offer for a counseling position at a women's crisis center. The pay was less than half of what Jasmine received and there sure weren't any stock options. Again, everything seemed easier for Jasmine.

When Jasmine announced her engagement last month, Monique cried for four days. She was angry because Jasmine's easy success has been an ongoing pattern throughout their lives and she was sick of it. Monique was also hurt. She had always suspected that Jasmine was her parents' favorite. Now she believed that God favored Jasmine over her, too. The words "It's just not fair" echo in Monique's mind.

UNHEALTHY COMPETITION

Rivalry-based envy is an intimate form of envy because it generally exists within a close relationship—between siblings, friends, or coworkers. Rivalry-based envy is different from the general and diffuse emotion of envy we may feel when we see something that triggers it. Rivalry adds another dimension to envy. A rival is someone whom we compare ourselves to and compete with (either consciously or unconsciously). We want to "top" them; we desire to outdo them. We struggle to be equal with our rival at the very least, but our preference is to beat them. The competition exists because the envious one believes that in "winning" she can be made whole. An interesting aspect of rivalry is that many times the rival is unaware that (1) they are an object of envy and (2) someone is in competition with them.

Of course, there is a harmless form of rivalry, such as two families who compete with each other every year at softball, or schools which vie for the basketball championship each year. There is the usual bragging—harmless threats of winning again next year—and good-natured taunting that takes place. That is not what we are talking about. The type of rivalry we are talking about is the intense competition that takes place within the envious person who desires victory to prove to themselves (or others) that they are sufficient.

Rivalry exists because the envious one believes that the rival has some unfair advantage, and therefore the rival possesses something desired. As we have seen earlier, one can envy anything. In the case of Monique and Jasmine, Monique desired what she perceived to be Jasmine's "easy life." For years, Monique felt that Jasmine had the unfair advantage, starting with her having to do less housework as a result of childhood asthma. It was probably irritating for Monique to see Jasmine relaxing while she worked around the house. Also, Monique expressed her suspicion that her parents favored her younger sister. Favoritism may or may not have existed, but because of the circumstances Monique believed it to be true. At the outset of the example, we were told that Monique and Jasmine constantly argued and bickered—which is an outcropping of rivalry. It is difficult to have a peaceful relationship with a rival because of the perception that they have an advantage over us. At the close, we see that Monique is frustrated, filled with resentment, and lamenting the unfairness of life.

JOSEPH—BEARING THE COST OF RIVALRY

An excellent biblical example of rivalry is found in Genesis 37. It is the account of a seventeen-year-old named Joseph, the second youngest of twelve brothers, who lived in the land of Canaan. Joseph was the rival of his brothers who grew to hate him. Let's take a look at some of the common traits that one finds in rivalry-based envy by looking at the life of Joseph.

Peer-Based
Rivalry-based envy usually occurs among peers—someone who is equal or similar to us. Our rivalry is with someone that we have things in common with or we know something about. For example,

I would not struggle with feelings of rivalry when comparing myself with the First Lady, the wife of the President of the United States. We are very dissimilar in that we have a different social circle, income, age, and life experiences. Nor do I have a chance to observe her intimately. If I had a rival, it would be someone whom I could observe, like a coworker or a neighbor.

In the example of Joseph, the rivalry was between him and his older brothers. Rivalry between siblings and friends is very common. According to William F. May, the author of *A Catalogue of Sins:*

> Envy enjoys a specific natural habitat. It finds itself most at home . . . in relations between equals.[2]

Suspected or Actual Favoritism
Another feature of rivalry-based envy is the perception of favor. Favor is when someone receives something extra or some sort of benefit because he or she is liked. Favoritism is the continuous and on-going state of having favor. This was the case with Joseph. He lived in an environment of constant favor over his brothers. Genesis 37:3 opens with the statement that "Israel loved Joseph more than any of his other sons, because he had been born to him in his old age." This favoritism is emphasized also at the opening of verse 4, which states, "When his brothers saw that their father loved him more than any of them, they hated him." It was clear to these brothers and is evident to a reader that there were problems in this family. It hurts to feel that someone is favored or preferred over us. Favoritism brings envy, and envy brings its running buddies—we met them in chapter 3: frustration, self-pity, grasping, and begrudging questioning.

Constant Irritation
Another feature of rivalry is that there is something about the rival that draws our attention to them. When we are envious, our attention is drawn to our rival because they possess something we want. Continually seeing them with what we desire becomes an irritant. The irritation occurs when we are sensitive to or desirous of something that we don't possess but our rival has, and that possession of what we desire annoys us. Envy becomes inflamed by "constant irritation" when the envious person sees the irritant on a

continual basis. In the case of Joseph, the constant irritant for his brothers was the coat his father gave him (Genesis 37:3). In some Bible translations, the coat is described as one having "many colors." In other translations, it is described as being richly "ornamented." Whatever the coat looked like, it was something to look at, and the brothers did so constantly. We can only imagine the hurt and frustration the brothers felt when they looked at the coats they wore and compared them to the coat their father had given to Joseph. It was a constant and ongoing reminder to them that their father loved Joseph more than he loved them.

There is also a second irritant mentioned in the Scriptures—Joseph was a tattletale. The Word says that Joseph brought back "bad reports" about his brothers to their father (Genesis 37:2); and in Genesis 37:12–14, we see that his father sent Joseph to check up on them. To the brothers, Joseph seemed like a spy in their midst. His very presence was an irritation.

Bad Attitude

A by-product of rivalry-based envy is having a bad attitude. We see in the Scriptures that the brothers "could not speak a kind word" to Joseph (Genesis 37:4), they hated him (v. 8), they were jealous of him (v. 11), they ridiculed him (v. 19), plotted to kill him (vv. 18, 20, 26), and in the end, they sold him into slavery (vv. 27, 28). When we have a bad attitude, we too have a hard time speaking a kind word to our rival. We can be defensive, rude, and challenging. We ridicule and pick apart our rival by finding fault with them, and we are quick to point out their shortcomings to others. Although most rivalries don't end in murder, they usually include a lot of character assassination.

At the heart of envy-based rivalry is the suspicion that our rival has some sort of advantage over us. Are they favored? Is God unfair? Is He guilty of shortchanging us?

8

FREE YOURSELF FROM TRAPPED THINKING: GOD IS UNFAIR

*Even though I was once a blasphemer
and a persecutor and a violent man,
I was shown mercy because
I acted in ignorance and unbelief.
The grace of our Lord was poured out
on me abundantly, along with the
faith and love that are in Christ Jesus.*
—I TIMOTHY 1:13–14

To be treated unfairly is a hard pill to swallow. It often leaves us feeling injured, helpless, and unhappy. It hurts when our every experience seems to end up with us getting the short end of every deal. Yet, no matter how hard we work and trust God for a balanced outcome, we end up getting plenty of outcome without the balance, lots of frustration without the fruition, and more bruises than blessings. To feel that we are being treated unfairly is something we all experience at various times in our lives. In addition, we can become overwhelmed when it seems as though everywhere we turn, life's occurrences reflect how unfair things are.

When an unfair outlook becomes a regular part of our daily life, the success of others also seems to reflect our failure. Their advances begin to reinforce how stuck we feel, and the blessings of others remind us of how hard we're working only to stay in the same place. When we begin to see signs that say "UNFAIR" posted at every turn, we become immobilized in our thinking and in our actions. Hopes and dreams fade fast. As a result, we begin to envy those we see, choose rivals from among those with whom we interact, and blame God for being unfair. We become trapped into believing that God is not on our side.

THE REASON FOR THE SEASON

The reason many of us get stuck in the season of having an outlook that proclaims "life is unfair" is because we get lost in the world of our own experiences. This means we become self-absorbed and have difficulty seeing beyond the scope of our own circumstances. No matter how hard we try, it seems we can only focus on what we don't have. At the same time, because we are struggling with intense desires, our mind is bombarded with thoughts of lack and lust. We are consumed within our own circumstances, and that causes us to lose our perspective of God, ourselves, and our situation. Next thing you know, everything we see points to the "fact" that our life is unfair. Even though we desire to view things in an objective manner, it is difficult to see things clearly. However, when you learn to view your life from God's perspective, your season will change.

GOD IS UNFAIR

The key to your freedom is knowing that God *is* unfair to us. This realization will only make sense if you understand His definition of the word *unfair.* Applying God's perspective of the word *unfair* will set you free. God's definition of the word *unfair* is "grace." Grace means that we receive more patience from God than we deserve. It means there is no limit to the number of times He forgives us. It says that He will love all of us, even the parts that don't deserve to be loved. The grace of God says, "I have given you everything you need in life to be successful and live for Me even though you deserve no life at all." Grace ultimately tells us that we don't have to die on the cross for our own sins (Colossians 2:13–15), because Jesus did that for you and me. It was unfair for Him to die, a sinless perfect man, but Jesus died in our place (Romans 5:6). God is full of grace, and He never runs out (1 Timothy 1:14). Therefore, grace is the promise (or agreement) that God makes with Himself that He will treat us unfairly—

that He will give us more than we really deserve. If God were fair, we would receive punishment, a life without Him, and eternal death. Aren't you glad that God is unfair?

So, how can your understanding of the fact that God treats us unfairly change your life? Well, when we understand that God *is* unfair, we are able to wipe out and replace our own harmful definition of what it means to be treated unfairly with His. Then we can *choose* to live life from His perspective. It is our choice to make. Instead of feeling that God has shortchanged us, we can understand that we have more than enough grace. Instead of feeling that everyone around us is "getting their's," we *choose* to open our eyes to what we do have. We decide to focus on the fact that God is present, active, and working in our lives. We make the choice to take more control over our thoughts by beginning to take on God's perspective. We start to live in His world, by focusing on His promises while living our lives with purpose that will bring Him glory. In other words, we choose to shift our focus from ourselves to our Savior. With this new outlook, we stop comparing ourselves to others; thus we end our search for rivals, and we can stop lugging the baggage of envy around with us. By shifting our focus, we can enter into a new season of life. Instead of feeling that life is unfair, we realize that we have more than enough grace to accomplish His will for our life (2 Corinthians 12:9).

9

BREAK THE
RIVALRY HABIT

But as for me, my feet had almost slipped;
I had nearly lost my foothold.
For I envied the arrogant
when I saw the prosperity of the wicked.
—PSALM 73:2–3

ASAPH'S ADVICE

Rivalry is habit-forming. We get used to observing our rival's life and comparing ourselves to them. We become accustomed to thinking about them from a fault-finding point of view. But rivalry-based envy is a habit that can be broken, and Psalm 73 gives us the key.

This psalm was written by Asaph, who was a Levite priest and musician during the reign of King David. Asaph also dealt with envy just as we do. In the psalm, Asaph shared with us who he envied: it was the arrogant and the wicked because he could see them prospering (Psalm 73:3). Asaph also felt that these evil people did not have the same burdens and problems as regular people—he felt that they had some type of advantage (vv. 4, 5, 12). Asaph describes the experience of "constant irritation" that comes with rivalry in verse 14a by stating, "All day long I have been plagued." It appears as though some ongoing frustration was weighing him down—so much so that Asaph felt he was being punished every morning (v. 14b). When he tried to make sense of his feelings, the situation, and life, even the process of trying to understand was oppressive to him (v. 16). As Asaph continued to observe the behavior of the wicked (vv. 6–11), he sums up what almost happened to him in Psalm 73:2:

But as for me, my feet had almost slipped; I had nearly lost my foothold.

Asaph's feelings are so real. Envy does cause us to slip, to suddenly lose our footing. This verse conjures up an image of walking outside on a frosty day, suddenly stepping on an icy patch of the sidewalk, involuntarily sliding and slipping, and flailing our arms to regain balance. Asaph paints that same picture of his feet starting to slide out from underneath him, his desire not to fall, and how he regained his balance. He shares with us how he regained his footing.

A CHANGE IN PERSPECTIVE

Asaph's turning point happens in Psalm 73:17. As you can see, there is a seamlessness between verses 16 and 17—it's really all one sentence. In verse 16, we see that he was trying to understand why things were the way they were; yet his conclusions, assumptions, or thoughts were too heavy for him. But in verse 17, Asaph says:

. . . till I entered the sanctuary of God; then I understood their final destiny.

The method for breaking the habit of rivalry involves getting before God and talking to Him. Ask Him to reveal Himself to you in a new way. Invite Him to show you life from His perspective. Ask Him to make known your destiny to you. In chapter 6, we talked about knowing your purpose and embracing your uniqueness. Knowing and moving toward your unique destiny sets you free from envy.

What is one's destiny? Our English word *destination* comes from the root word *destine*. An easy way to describe our destiny is to use the *Webster's Ninth New Collegiate Dictionary* definition of "destination" which is the place to which one is journeying. Where are you heading in life? What is your final destination? What will be your legacy after you leave this earth?

When thinking of destiny, Ecclesiastes 3:11 comes to mind:

> He [God] has made everything beautiful in its **time**. He has also set **eternity** in the **hearts** of men; yet they cannot fathom what God has done from beginning to end.

The three components of destiny are in this Scripture: time, eternity, and our hearts. Destiny is accomplished over *time*; it affects *eternity*; but first, our destiny is birthed in our *hearts*. These three concepts are key components to victory over envy—because envy hinders us and keeps us from fulfilling our destiny. Let's take a look at each of these components of destiny and see how remembering them can help us conquer envy.

Time

We are creatures locked in a dimension called time. We experience the measured, linear sensation of the passage of time. We only have a certain amount of time because our days are numbered (Psalm 139:15–16). We measure time by years, months, days, hours, minutes, and seconds. But when we look at someone else's life, we are just looking at *"a snapshot in time."* No matter how well or how long we know someone, we do not know all of their days.

When I was in my twenties, I had a friend whose life I had observed for about three years, and I envied her. I thought her life was so wonderful and easy. But I didn't know her full days. It wasn't until I got to know her better that I discovered that she had a rough childhood, *and* she had some very difficult years after that three-year period. But because I had met her during that season of her life, I had presupposed her whole life was wonderful. What I saw of her life was just a snapshot in a certain frame of time.

Rivalry-based envy makes assumptions about people. It assumes that things have always been as they are today and that they will stay that way into the future. Even if we have observed someone's life for years, we are still only seeing a segment of their life because we don't know the future. We certainly don't know the twists and turns people's lives will take. What we envy today may be God blessing them now to prepare them for possible hard times in the future. The bottom line is we don't know what that person needs or why God is blessing them. But realizing that we're only seeing a *"snapshot in time"* helps us relinquish our desire to judge whether or not someone *deserves* what they have or not. Realizing that we do not see the whole picture from beginning to end helps us to surrender our critiques of other people's lives. By turning the focus off of others, we are allowing God to be God in their life and ours.

Eternity

What is eternity? It is more than just a designer fragrance. Eternity is outside of fixed, measured time. It has no beginning nor does it have an end—it just is . . . forever. Our souls and our spirits are eternal, but our bodies are not. After our bodies die, our spirit and our soul (our mind, will, and emotions) live on forever—outside of time. The Bible says that for the Lord, a thousand years are just like one day going by (Psalm 90:4). But for us, our days are compared to grass and the wind passes over us and we are no more (Psalm 103:15–16). So how do we reconcile our concept of time with the Lord's concept of time? Since God says that He does not change (Malachi 3:6), it is up to us to *"surrender our timing."*

Achieving victory over envy requires that we yield our timing. Many times we envy others for the things we want for ourselves right now but don't have yet. We always have a good idea of when we want things done. We have a fixed measurement of time set in our minds by which we want certain things accomplished. We want it NOW! But it is for our protection and benefit to yield our timing to the Lord. In fact, our ability to receive God's best plan for our lives is directly linked to our willingness to submit to God's timing. Daniel 2:20–22 says:

> *Praise be to the name of God forever and ever; wisdom and power are his. He changes times and seasons; he sets up kings and deposes them. He gives wisdom to the wise and knowledge to the discerning. He reveals deep and hidden things; he knows what lies in darkness, and light dwells with him.*

The biggest mistakes of our lives are made by not waiting for God.

We get entangled with situations that we should never have been in because we could not see "what lies in darkness." But God sees everything because He has all wisdom and power. When we wait on Him and for His timing, He reveals to us things we had no way of knowing on our own. He is our protection when we are paying attention to Him. But the exciting part of this Scripture is that it is God who changes times and seasons. And He raises and lowers people. By waiting on God for His appropriate timing, by asking Him to reveal hidden things and believing that He can set you up for your blessing, you can have victory over envy.

Our Hearts
The Bible says that what is in our heart comes right out of our mouths (Matthew 12:34). When we are envious, we are believing life is good for someone else and bad for us. In other words, when we envy others, we also have the tendency to say negative things about ourselves and our situation. We must *guard against demeaning self-talk*. Many times, it's not what others say to us that hurts; it's what we say *to and about* ourselves that causes the greatest injury.

What is self-talk? It is those things that we say to ourselves, sometimes in our thoughts and other times out loud. It's what you say to yourself when you are muttering or grumbling. It is those things that we believe to be true about our life and our situation. Do you believe your girlfriend married the last nice man on the planet or that there are not enough good men around? That's self-talk. Are all men dogs? Are all of them only after one thing? Do you believe you're too old, too plain, or too heavy to get married? That's self-talk. Become alert to your self-talk because your words have power. The Bible says if you believe what you say, then that is what you will have (Mark 11:23). If what you are saying is not what you want for the rest of your life, start changing what you say.

LIVE YOUR DREAMS

The most important key to obtaining victory over envy is to go forth and live your dreams. *Do things that bring you pleasure.* Break the rivalry habit by putting your focus on what you have always wanted. What brings you pleasure? What have you always wanted to do?

Many times when we are in competition with someone else, the very thing we envy about them is a signal to us that there is something missing in our lives. For example, you envy a friend who decided she wanted to live in Paris. She saved her money, quit her job, and the next thing you know, she's winging her way to France and you're envious. Perhaps your feelings of envy are a signal that you haven't taken enough chances in life to pursue your own dreams.

Don't put off living your dreams because you are waiting for a man or marriage. When I was single, one of the biggest and best decisions I made was to go forward and buy my own home. For years I had struggled with that question because I had already pictured in my mind that my husband and I would choose our first home together. After years of waiting for him to come along, I *finally* came to the decision that I needed to get my own home—by myself. I never regretted it. If a man I dated thought it was "too intimidating" that I owned my own home by myself—he was not the man for me. I decorated, I painted, I learned about plumbing, I gardened, and I grew as a person. Another five years passed before I met my husband, and one of the things he liked about me was that I owned a home.

Do you need a larger place to be comfortable? If it's financially feasible for you, go ahead and move. Have you always wanted to learn how to ride a horse? Go take lessons. Get yourself beautiful dishes and eat off of them now. Have you always wanted to read your poetry out loud but hesitated to do so? Take the chance. Go to a coffee house with an open mike, bring your poems, and read them to others. Don't save your pretty towels and sheets until you're married. Use them now because you alone are worth it. Volunteer! Worthy organizations are always looking for help. Cut some flowers and have fresh flowers in your home. Adopt—there are so many children who need someone to love them. Buy and wear pretty underwear—it makes you feel good about yourself. Make it your goal to check on an elderly neighbor once a week and play checkers or cards with them. Stop talking about going back to school and do it! Go get your A.A., your B.A., your M.A., or your Ph.D.

Go and live *your* life! Get your eyes off of others and LIVE!

STRATEGIC MOVES

1. List five things you have always wanted to do.

2. Choose one of the items on your list and either make a plan to do it or take steps to achieve it.

DISCOURAGEMENT

10

THE WEIGHT
OF DISCOURAGEMENT

Even in laughter the heart may ache.
—PROVERBS 14:13

PAYING THE PIPER

Suzette is thirty-six, single again, and teetering on the edge of bankruptcy. Her ex-husband, Jazz, loved two things: his saxophone and spending money. He maxed-out their credit cards and then told Suzette that he and the band were going on tour to make some money. At first she heard from him, a phone call here and there. Also, every so often, he would send her a couple hundred dollars. No return addresses on the envelopes but postmarks from Las Vegas, Phoenix, El Paso, Texarkana, Arkadelphia, and after St. Louis, nothing. The bottom line is Jazz has disappeared. Now newly divorced, Suzette is stuck paying off the bills because her name also appeared on the accounts. Although she's been paying the debts for the last year and a half, she still owes $14,000. She's discouraged and is ready to give up.

WHAT IS DISCOURAGEMENT?

Discouragement is the heavy feeling of sadness that comes as a result of losing hope. It's the feeling we experience when we're faced with a situation in which we have tried everything we can think of and we're not sure where to turn next. Discouragement is different from frustration in that on the edges of frustration is anger, but on the fringes of discouragement is sadness and hopelessness.

According to *Webster's Ninth New Collegiate Dictionary,* the word *discouragement* comes from an old French word *descoragier* which means to "deprive of courage;" the root word being *corage* which means "courage" in English.[1] The root French word for "courage" comes from the word *cuer,* which means "heart." It was believed that it was the area of the heart from which we drew our strength, resilience, and courage. When someone was very brave or persistent under adverse circumstances, it was said that person had "heart." The "dis" prefix means to separate. Therefore, "discouragement" means to separate one from their courage. The word "dishearten" is a similar word that we also use to describe the act of discouraging someone.

To be discouraged means that our circumstances cause us to lose heart. In other words, our strength, daring, and our "can-do" attitude disappear. Discouragement occurs when our courage dissolves in the face of opposition. It's like being in a ring with a highly skilled opponent who has outboxed you in the first two rounds. Now it's round three of the fight and your body aches, your nose is bleeding, and your arms are so tired they feel like dead weights. You are intimidated, and you don't want to leave your corner for the next round. You're feeling anxious, and you're tired of fighting because your opponent appears unstoppable. You're feeling discouraged.

DISCOURAGEMENT VERSUS DEPRESSION

Each of us has been discouraged at one time or another. We have gone a round or two with negative circumstances and we felt beat up. But when does discouragement cross the line to depression? It occurs when your feelings of discouragement begin to interfere with your ability to work or maintain satisfactory relationships with those around you. That's when you know you're moving into something more serious—like depression. Let's take a look at the difference between some practical signs of discouragement and depression.

What's Affected	What Discouragement Says	What Depression Says
Ability to Function	"I'm disappointed, but I'm able to go on with my day."	"I can't get out of bed."
Loss of Interest and Lack of Social Desire	"I don't feel like going to the movies with my friends, but I'll go anyway."	"Even though it's my favorite thing to do, I'm not interested in going."
Appetite	"Yes, I'm unhappy but my appetite is unchanged."	"More food or no food."
Sleep Habits	"Life is not what I want it to be— but I sleep well anyway."	"Life hurts— so I sleep to escape or I hardly sleep at all."

Along with the feelings of depression come a lack of energy, the inability to concentrate, and the feelings of worthlessness or futility that directly and negatively affect our work and relationships.

Another symptom of depression has to do with the length of time one has been in a "down" mood. If a person is in a low mood most of the time—suffering from insomnia or sleeping too much, has lost interest in things that used to give them pleasure, has a distinct lack of energy, can't concentrate, or is having thoughts of killing themselves—the chances of them being depressed increases as the number of symptoms increase. If these symptoms have lasted two or more weeks, it is very important to contact a medical professional immediately and get a full physical exam. By sharing the symptoms with your doctor, he or she can provide the necessary guidance. Also, if you know someone who fits this description of depression—reach out to them, be understanding, and encourage them to get professional, physical, or psychological assistance.

IT HAPPENS TO ALL OF US

Everyone experiences discouragement. There are intimidating circumstances that women face on a daily basis that become discouraging because of the duration of the challenging situation. In other words, some women have been fighting the same battle, possibly for years, and the span of time has become disheartening. Discouragement also comes because our circumstances are overwhelming. We are bombarded by so many things at the same time that we can feel as though we are drowning. Some of us become discouraged because of repeated disappointment, and others because of misplaced affection—investing our love in the "wrong" person. Are you discouraged?

QUIZ: ARE YOU WEIGHED DOWN BY DISCOURAGEMENT?

Instructions: Answer "True" or "False" to describe how you feel about your life **most of the time.**

1. I feel down or sad about some aspect of my life.

2. When I look at my circumstances I wonder "why me?"

3. I feel that God has let me down.

4. I currently feel overwhelmed with my life.

5. I feel reluctant to try new things because they probably won't work out.

6. My dreams, goals, and desires are elusive.

7. I am repeatedly disappointed in my life.

8. I put people in the place of God to meet my needs.

9. I feel God doesn't answer my prayers.

Scoring: If you answered "True" to two or more questions, it is possible that you are discouraged.

I'M DROWNING: DISCOURAGED BY OVERWHELMING CIRCUMSTANCES

As they sailed, he [Jesus] fell asleep.
A squall came down on the lake,
so that the boat was being swamped,
and they were in great danger.
The disciples went and woke him, saying,
"Master, Master, we're going to drown!"
—LUKE 8:23–24

DROWNING

Keta has two children, each with different fathers. Her baby girl's father hasn't paid child support in nine months because he lost his job, but at least he stops by; she hasn't seen her son's father in four years. She is twenty-six years old, and she works at the hospital eight hours a day with a half hour for lunch. The pay is low, the work is tedious, and there doesn't seem to be a way to move up from her current position. The rent on her one-bedroom apartment just increased fifty dollars a month and it is due in three days. Even though she's working, she never seems to have enough money. Between the baby-sitter, rent, utilities, groceries, and insurance—she can't make ends meet. The lady who keeps her children told Keta that this coming Friday will be the last day, so she needs to find someone fast to take care of them.

Keta wishes she could call her mother, but it's been a month since they have spoken. Her mother told her she was tired of always bailing Keta out by giving her money or baby-sitting all the time. She also said that Keta was in this mess because she didn't want to listen to anybody—so she could just lie in the bed she made. That last comment really hurt. Keta knows she's made some mistakes, but she's not sure what to do next. She wants to do better, but she doesn't know how. The weight of her responsibilities seems overwhelming, and she feels discouraged.

THE LIFE OF TODAY'S WOMAN

Keta is drowning. One of the major causes of discouragement among single women is the feeling of being overwhelmed. Like so many women today, Keta is under pressure and overwhelmed by responsibilities. She is representative of women who are:

- hardworking, yet find it difficult to make ends meet
- single parents with very little outside support
- stuck on a treadmill with no end in sight

You don't have to be a single parent to feel overwhelmed. Everyone feels disheartened in the face of daily opposition in our regular routines. Discouragement sets in when the overly scheduled day begins to drain your body, mind, and spirit. It's when that panicky drowning sensation arrives because we have too much on our plate, but we're too exhausted to do anything about it.

Women who are single parents can be particularly susceptible to discouragement as a result of being overwhelmed. The demands of being the sole provider and having the unshared responsibility for the maintenance and care of children can be, and oftentimes is, overwhelming. Because of the lack of a support system, single women attempt to be both mother and father; it is an attempt which often leads to fatigue, guilt, loneliness, and discouragement.

IT'S ALL ABOUT OUR SPIRIT

We become discouraged when our spiritual, physical, and mental/emotional reserves become depleted. We are triune (three-part) beings: we are spirits, who live in a body, and have a soul (which is comprised of our mind, will, and emotions). It is easy for us to recognize when our physical reserves become depleted. When we are hungry, we eat; when we get tired, we sleep; when we are thirsty, we get something to drink. But do we recognize when the reserves for our spirit and our soul are used up? Just as our bodies send signals warning us of hunger, tiredness, or thirst, likewise, our spirit transmits the message that it, too, needs refreshing.

Discouragement is the signal from our spirit that we need to replenish the reserves. Because we are spirit beings, our spirit impacts our body and our soul. That means when our spirit is depleted, it affects the way our body feels, the way we think, the emotions we feel, and our will (our internal fortitude and strength). When we're feeling discouraged, our minds can become overly anxious, and we can't concentrate; we're irritable, exhausted, and without hope. Combating discouragement involves replenishing our spirits, giving peace to our souls, and taking care of our bodies. However, before we get to the solution, we need to identify the specific cause(s) of our discouragement.

ONGOING OR SUDDEN OR BOTH?

The discouragement that results from being overwhelmed often follows two basic types of life circumstances: ongoing or sudden. An "ongoing" situation is a continuous occurrence or circumstance that has not ceased, nor is there an end in sight. In a "sudden" circumstance, something unexpected was added to our already heavy load; it's kind of like that last straw—the one that broke the camel's back. For most of us, discouragement is triggered by a combination of both sudden and ongoing circumstances. For example, Keta had the ongoing circumstance of being a single parent, employed in a dead-end job, struggling with financial troubles. But two sudden circumstances triggered the feeling of discouragement: the fifty dollar rent increase and the abrupt loss of child care support. Keta is overwhelmed and discouraged. What kind of circumstances are you dealing with in your life right now?

ARE YOU OVERWHELMED?

How many of these circumstances are occurring in your life? Check off all that apply.

_____ Going to school while working

_____ Forced overtime

_____ Breakup of relationship

_____ Layoffs threatened

_____ Increase in utility bills

_____ Stressful work

_____ Behind in mortgage or rent

_____ High car payments

_____ Loss or lack of transportation

_____ Dead-end job

_____ Single parenting

_____ Long commute

_____ Surviving recent disaster—earthquake, tornado, etc.

_____ Assisting elderly parents

_____ Getting less than six hours of sleep per night

_____ Demanding boss

_____ Loss of a friendship

_____ Constant colds

_____ Car mechanical problems

_____ Sick child

_____ Constant criticism

_____ No "down time" or opportunity for self-care

_____ School loan payments

_____ A large project

_____ Personal health challenge

_____ Loss of job

_____ Legal problems or having to testify in court

_____ Tight deadlines

_____ Death in family

_____ Credit card debts

_____ Daily pressure to pick up children from day care by a certain time

_____ Lack of financial child support

_____ Indecisive or concerned about personal future

_____ Loneliness

_____ Lack of consistent child care

_____ Rent increase

_____ Unexpected bills

_____ Daily meal preparation

_____ Living with clutter or in a disorganized home

_____ Victim of crime

_____ Other _____

_____ Other _____

Any one of the above items, depending on the intensity, can bring on discouragement. However, many of us deal with these types of stressors all at the same time. So what do you do with the discouragement that you feel as a result of being over-whelmed? Does God really care that you're overwhelmed? Let's take a look.

12

FREE YOURSELF FROM TRAPPED THINKING: GOD DOESN'T CARE

The LORD himself goes before you
and will be with you;
He will never leave you nor forsake you.
Do not be afraid; do not be discouraged.
—DEUTERONOMY 31:8

Heavy feelings of sadness, frustrated efforts, overwhelming circumstances, and the effects of discouragement can not only make you wonder if anyone cares; they could also cause you to ask if God cares: "After all, why would He allow me to feel 'the weight of the world' without any help?"

ISOLATION

Discouragement can be a very lonely feeling because it often leads to isolation. When we are isolated, it is easy to believe that nobody cares, including God. Isolation can be physical or emotional. We may either stay in the house and rarely come out (physical isolation) or not share our inner pain with anyone (emotional isolation). When discouragement leads to isolation, we lessen our contact with family, friends, and the outside world. What we don't realize is that not only does discouragement lead to physical and emotional isolation;

it also leads to spiritual isolation as well. We generally don't compartmentalize our isolation. When we run or hide from family, friends, or society, we carry the same behavior into our relationship with God. We hide from Him, too. When we run from Him, He seems far away. And when He feels distant we ask, "Does God care?"

HE CARES FOR YOU

The beauty of the Bible is that no matter what we go through in life that causes us to think incorrectly about God (or ourselves), we can always go to His Word and allow God to correct our thinking. There are hundreds of Scriptures throughout the Bible that support the fact that God loves and cares for you. However, there is one Scripture in particular that not only reminds us that God cares, but gives us instructions on how to experience His care even in the midst of the anxiety that often accompanies discouragement, isolation, and feeling overwhelmed. That verse is 1 Peter 5:7, which says:

Cast all your anxiety on him because he cares for you.

Notice He does not say, "*If* you cast your anxiety on Me *then* I will care for you." Rather He says, "Cast your anxiety on Me *because* I *already* care for you." That's right! In the middle of your trials and troubles, God has never stopped caring for you. The problem is, when we are discouraged, the weight of the baggage we are carrying distracts us from being able to experience God's care. We were never designed to carry our own emotional or spiritual burdens. Instead, God wants us to experience His care, but first, He wants us to drop the weights. We eliminate the baggage by casting all of our anxiety on Him. When you do this, you clear the path for you to experience His ever-present love—His care that was always there for you.

CAST YOUR CARE

The Greek word for "cast" in 1 Peter 5:7 is *epi,* which means to rest upon, or in motion toward. Whether you have become overtaken by your circumstances or are overwhelmed because you are trying to do it all yourself, God wants you to cast all your problems onto

Him. He wants you to experience His care by putting all that concerns you "in motion toward" Him so He can handle it. He wants to carry your load. But first, you must learn how to cast.

The best fishermen are those who perfect the technique of casting. When a fisherman makes a cast, the first thing he does is release the bail of his reel so the fishing line can flow freely. As he flicks his wrist and flings his pole forward, he causes his hook, line, and sinker (weight) to arch away from him. It briefly flies through the air and lands several yards away from him to enter the water where, hopefully, the fish are swimming. However, in order for a fisherman to make a good cast to where the big fish are, he must put a weight at the end of the fishing line. The heavier the weight, the farther he can cast.

God doesn't mind taking on the weight of your problems, no matter how heavy. In fact, the more weight (problems) you have, the farther you can cast your problems onto God. Just as a fisherman throws his sinker as far as he can, God wants you to cast the weight of your problems onto Him. This way you can experience His loving care. Whether it's a stressful job, family struggles, legal problems, or financial challenges, learn how to cast all your care onto Him. The more problems you cast onto Him, the more you can experience His care. Break the power of discouragement and isolation by casting your cares onto Him.

STRATEGY FOR PEACE

Cast your burden. Casting your cares takes practice, so practice your casting skills every day.

1. Create a list of items that you want to cast.

2. Cast each one to God by praying. Your prayer can be something like this:

Lord, I give name the problem(s) to You. It is not mine to carry because You delight in carrying my burdens. You can carry my problem(s) better than I can. Because I have given this to You to carry, I can experience Your care for me. I thank You, in the name of Jesus.

3. Thank God regularly for taking care of the problem. Giving thanks is your reminder that you have given it to Him to carry for good.

CHAPTER

13

SUBDUE OVERWHELMING CIRCUMSTANCES

*May God himself, the God of peace,
sanctify you through and through.
May your whole spirit, soul and body be kept
blameless at the coming of our Lord Jesus Christ.*
—I THESSALONIANS 5:23

As we saw in chapter 11, we are three-part beings. We are a spirit who lives in a body and has a soul. We also learned that discouragement is a signal from our spirit telling us that we need to be rejuvenated. Most of us get in trouble in that we try to renew only one or two parts of ourselves. So we escape on a vacation and we may relax our body and our mind, but our spirit is still depleted. A week later, we are still discouraged. The key to subduing overwhelming circumstances is to rejuvenate all three areas of your being, and in the process, tackle your situation. Let's start with the most important part of yourself first.

YOUR SPIRIT

Your spirit is the source of your physical, mental, and emotional strength and stability, so it is important to take care of your spirit first when you are facing overwhelming circumstances.

- **Talk to God**—Share with Him what you are going through. Invite Him into your situation. Ask Him for wisdom to handle your circumstance. After all, God has promised to give wisdom freely to all who ask Him for it (James 1:5).
- **Listen to God's Answer**—Sit quietly and wait for God to speak to you. How? Most times, He speaks to us through His printed Word. Start by reading His Word. There will be times when particular parts of the Scriptures will seem to leap off the page at you and the words go straight to your heart. That's when you've heard from God. His Holy Spirit puts that life-spark into His words. Other times, God speaks to us in a still, gentle voice. Take time and wait for Him to speak. As Terri Mc-Fadden said in her sermon "Your Relationship with God" on May 5, 2001, at the Alhatti Christian Resort, "God is not a cheap date." You have to invest yourself in the relationship if you want to hear from Him.
- **Eat Spiritual Food**—Just as our physical body needs physical food, our spiritual body needs spiritual food. Therefore, we need to systematically feed our spirits the Word of God by reading our Bible, repeating verses out loud, and trying to memorize them.
- **Eliminate Junk**—That means turn off the television. Give your spirit a vacation from all the negativity that is transmitted on a daily basis. Turn off the television and particularly stop watching the news. The news seems to gather all the bad events from around the world and tell us as much about them as it can in a thirty-minute segment. Actually, the news can be quite over-whelming, especially if it taps into fears and anxieties you may already be feeling. Stop watching the news for a season. Also, be aware of the kind of music you're listening to. Is it building up your spirit or are the artists singing about heartbreak, trials, and bitterness? Add gospel music to your listening repertoire. Hear about the goodness of the Lord instead of some junk.

PHYSICAL BODY

When you are discouraged as a result of living with overwhelming circumstances, you need to take extra care of your body. When we are discouraged, we ignore our bodies and they get very run down. That's part of the reason why we may not be feeling 100 percent.

- **Get a Physical Exam**—When dealing with prolonged stress and overwhelming circumstances, it's important for you to get your body checked out by your doctor. Women of color usually don't take the time or have the access to good medical care. We often go years without a thorough physical exam. Please, whatever you have to do to be seen by a doctor, just do it. And before you go for your visit, write out a list of questions or complaints so you can have your questions handy. See a doctor, as soon as you can.
- **Get More Sleep**—According to *American Demographics* (January 1999 issue), people who get six or less hours of sleep a night have a 70 percent higher mortality rate. Do what you can to get to bed earlier.
- **Exercise**—This is the most wonderful gift you can give yourself. Even just doing some simple stretches can invigorate you and improve your mood.

BUILDING UP YOUR SOUL

Your soul encompasses your mind, your will, and your emotions. Each of these three areas need attention.

Your Mind
When you are discouraged due to overwhelming circumstances, your mind may be an untapped reservoir of ideas. But because the situation may be chaotic, you may not have had the opportunity to do some practical problem-solving exercises to bring your circumstances under control. Here are a few suggestions:

- **A Master-Mind Group**—This is where you invite a group of trusted friends to meet with you, and you clearly (and honestly) share with them your situation. Then everyone brainstorms solutions. Write down all of the ideas no matter how crazy or unusual because there are no bad ideas. Afterwards, discuss the practicality of each idea. This method should give you a couple of fresh ideas to apply to your situation.

- **Prioritize**—Oftentimes, when we're overwhelmed, everything seems urgent. But the reality is that some things are less urgent than others, and some are just time wasters. Prioritize your activities. Put the items that "must be done now" in order of importance, and separate them from things that are "nice to do" but are not necessary. By prioritizing your time, you will actually be able to accomplish the most important things and thereby gradually eliminate time wasters. Get a good time-management book to help you in this area.

- **Bite-Sized Pieces**—Divide up a large, overwhelming project into smaller pieces. For example, you want to clean out the clutter in your home. Rather than thinking about cleaning your *whole* house, divide it up into "bite-sized pieces." One way to do that is to divide your time. Set the buzzer for thirty minutes, vigorously clean for only the half hour, and then stop until the next day. If you clean for a half an hour, it's not enough time to get bogged down in the tedium of the task. Yet if you cleaned for a half an hour on the weekdays and increased it to an hour on the weekends, you will gradually make progress in cleaning your home. Another way to accomplish the task of de-cluttering is to divide up your home. For example, rather than having to clean the whole house, just do one closet, one drawer, or one corner at a time. Only clean that one area and then stop for the day. You get the picture.

Your Will

Our will is that "want-to" part of us. It is where we express our desires and make our choices. It's where our willingness or reluctance to do something resides. Our will plays quite a role in helping us to conquer discouragement.

- **Want to Change**—You must first have the desire to change the behavior that leads to becoming overwhelmed. Are your expectations too high about what can be accomplished each day? Then you must *want to* work on expectations. Have you made poor choices that have impacted your circumstance?

Then you must *want to* learn how to make better choices. Is your circumstance a result of prior financial misjudgments? Then you must *want to* learn to manage money differently. We must *want to* change to escape discouragement.

• **Ask for Help**—Make the decision to reach out and ask others for assistance. We all need help at one time or another. An extra pair of hands to come alongside of us can not only give us needed assistance, but encouragement too.

• **Learn to Say "No"**—Part of subduing overwhelming circumstances is to cut out unnecessary items. You just can't be everywhere and do everything for everyone. By saying "no" you can avoid the inevitable resentment that accompanies not wanting to be somewhere or having to do something you do not want to or have time to do.

Your Emotions

Our feelings are very important, and we can't ignore how we feel. However, when we're discouraged, it is often difficult to untangle and identify the many emotions we may be experiencing. The following suggestion may help:

• **Talk to Someone**—When you are discouraged, it is so important to have someone to talk to, someone who will allow you to vent and express the frustration you are feeling. That person can be any "safe" person with whom you feel comfortable—a friend, relative, lay counselor, or a professional therapist. The important thing is that you get an opportunity to express and explore your feelings.

• **Journal**—Writing is a great way to express your feelings. The wonderful thing about keeping a journal is that it causes you to identify tangled feelings, because you are forced to give them a name in order to write about them. Keeping a journal can be a wonderful, lifelong habit.

These are just a few suggestions. The bottom line is: to conquer discouragement, you must allow God to work through all parts of your being—your spirit, your soul, and your body.

CHAPTER

14

DISCOURAGED BECAUSE I'VE BEEN DISAPPOINTED— AGAIN

In bitterness of soul Hannah
wept much and prayed to the Lord . . .
saying, "O LORD Almighty, if you will only look
upon your servant's misery and remember me . . ."
—I SAMUEL 1:10–11

TIME AFTER TIME

After three broken engagements, Annette is discouraged. The first engagement was to Nick, the summer after she graduated from high school. Even though they knew they were going to separate colleges, they figured their love would last until they graduated. It didn't. She concluded that they were too young anyway. Her second engagement occurred in her late twenties. It ended after she discovered that he had a gambling addiction. But this engagement was different. She and Jeff truly loved each other, and Annette believed that *this time* she was really getting married.

Almost two years ago Annette met Jeff on a blind date, and a year later he proposed. However, within the last couple of months, Annette has noticed that Jeff has been distant. She would try to engage him in conversation to find out what was bothering him, but he would just shrug and say nothing was wrong or that he had a hard day. Last week her fears were confirmed when he broke off the engagement saying that he "just wasn't ready for marriage." Even though she knew his behavior had changed, the breakup was still a shock and a huge disappointment. Annette really thought she had met the man of her dreams. Instead, she's thirty-eight, has a non-refundable wedding gown, and has a box of unmailed invitations. What's even worse is having to explain to family and friends that she's not getting married—again. Annette is discouraged and profoundly disappointed.

It's different for Renee. Her disappointment isn't over one major thing; it's the continual series of small, everyday disappointments that she finds discouraging. She's a nurse and has been praying to get off the night shift for five months—she's still there. Renee prayed for the mechanic to discover why her car kept stalling—after $200 for repair work, it still stalls. She prayed about finding an escort to a wedding of a friend; everyone was busy that day, so she went alone. When Renee looks back over her life, she realizes that it has been filled with a series of disappointments. It seems that whenever she wants something, she doesn't get it. Renee prays, yet she feels her prayers go unheard. Renee is discouraged because she feels that God does not care about her needs.

GREAT EXPECTATIONS

Disappointment seems to come in different sizes. Some are delivered to us in big refrigerator-sized boxes like Annette's broken engagement, while others come in a variety of smaller-sized boxes. Some of us receive a series of "small" disappointments all at once; others get large destiny-altering disappointments. But whether our delivery of disappointment is frequent or rare, all of us receive these "special deliveries."

Disappointment is the emotion we feel when what we desire disappears, slips away, or is otherwise unavailable to us. Disappointment occurs when we expect to possess or receive something, and we are permanently or temporarily separated from it. Disappointment is the feeling that happens when hope dies. It's the sadness that follows the death of an expectation. Disappointment is a form of mourning that comes when something inside dies.

We can also experience disappointment when something is not as nice as we would like it to be. For example, many years ago a friend of mine received tickets to a $100-a-plate dinner—it was a political fund-raiser. Since neither of us had ever gone to such an expensive event, we were expecting something fabulous. When we arrived at the appointed location, it turned out to be at an ordinary-looking restaurant/bar. At first we thought we were at the wrong location, but we ran into other people in the parking lot looking as confused as we were. Once inside, all of the guests were hustled into the bar portion of the facility where we sat for over an hour waiting for them to get prepared. After a lukewarm dinner, we were subjected to political speeches which were quite "unique"—so much so that there was audible chuckling from the audience. By the end of the evening, we were relieved to leave, but very disappointed about the caliber of the event. The dinner did not live up to our expectations.

There is a relationship between disappointment and expectation. Our degree of disappointment has a direct correlation to our level of expectation. The higher our expectations, the harsher our disappointment. We all know about this tie between hope and disappointment, even if it's on a subconscious level; that's why when something wonderful is about to happen, we try not to get our hopes up. We do our best to stifle our excitement about the possibilities because we realize that the higher our expectation, the greater our possible disappointment. Even those around us caution us with well-meaning phrases like:

"I wouldn't get too excited if I were you ..."
"Don't get your hopes up ..."
"Let's wait and see what will happen first ..."

In fact, we really don't need to hear these statements from others, because we are already saying them to ourselves. Many of us are more familiar with the feeling of disappointment than the feeling of hope.

STRATEGIC MOVES

1. What disappointment have you experienced?

2. Why do you think you were so disappointed?

3. How did you usually handle hope?

4. Do you enjoy being hopeful or do you try to avoid getting your hopes up?

THE CHALLENGE OF KEEPING HOPE ALIVE

Hope is like a delicate flowering plant. When we receive this plant, we discover that it must be kept in the shade, protected from pests, and frequently watered. If any one of these instructions is not followed, this beautiful plant will not flourish. The same is true of hope—it too requires protection from the harsh sunlight, safekeeping from pests, and plenty of water. For example, sometimes we purposefully place the little shade-loving hope plant in the brutal sunlight to wither and die. This generally occurs when we have experienced many disappointments in the past and we decide to make our lives "easier" by killing off hope so we won't have to experience the disappointment that inevitably comes if things don't work out. Other times our delicate hope plant is killed off by pests. That's when circumstances gnaw and nibble away at our hope until we watch it die before our eyes. Many times our little hope plant just dries up because we forget to water it. We water the flowering plant of hope the more we think and pray about the possibility of the dream coming to pass.

Without the proper protection, hope dies. And regardless of *how* hope dies, the results are the same. Without hope, there is a heaviness to life, a weariness that causes us to mope. We feel fearful about our future, despondent, and pessimistic about life. It is when we are without hope that we willingly sacrifice our personal boundaries and emotional well-being to desperately clutch at something or someone we perceive will deliver us from our hopelessness. We involve ourselves in unhealthy relationships. When we are without hope, we have a pain called "worldly sorrow"—that is the pain leading to death because 2 Corinthians 7:10 says:

> *Godly sorrow brings repentance that leads to salvation and leaves no regret, but worldly sorrow brings death.*

If our pain doesn't bring us to salvation, then it is "worldly sorrow" leading to death. If our sorrow in hopelessness isn't drawing us closer to God and bringing us into right relationship with Him, it is leading us to death, which is spiritual separation from God.

So it appears as though we are caught between a rock and a hard place. We avoid hope because it hurts; however, choosing to live a life without hope leads to worldly sorrow which brings with it death. But if we choose hope, it seems that we are also choosing pain. We know from experience that with hope comes the possible pain of disappointment. If hope can cause such pain and suffering, that leads us to question the value of hope.

IS HOPE A GOOD THING?

"Is hope a good thing?" one might ask. Absolutely! Hope gives life. Hope actually fosters healthy feelings in us. When we're hopeful about something, we have joy, enthusiasm, confidence, and self-assurance. Hope gives us the desire to set goals and the aspirations to accomplish our objectives. We actually take more risks in life, daring to stretch forward to try new things, when we have hope. We hold our heads up high and we have a bounce in our step when we are secure in the knowledge that success is possible—when we feel that our dreams can come true. We become excited about life because we have confidence that our desire can be attained. Besides all of these things, God wants us to have hope.

God clearly communicates through the Bible what His will is *for* us and His intentions are *toward* us. And one of the things He wants us to know is that He wants us to put our hope in Him. It makes Him happy when we hope in Him and believe the best about Him; He says so in Psalm 147:11:

> . . . *the* LORD *delights in those who fear him, who put their hope in His unfailing love.*

In 1 Timothy 6:17, God also cautions us not to hope in the things that are in our lives:

> *Command those who are rich in this present world not to be arrogant nor to put their hope in wealth, which is so uncertain, but to put their hope in God.*

Maybe you don't think that this Scripture applies to you because you are not financially wealthy. However, we are "rich in this present world," particularly if we live in a country where there is freedom. God also wants us to be confident that He has our best interests in His heart. He communicates this truth in Jeremiah 29:11:

> *"For I know the plans I have for you," declares the* LORD, *"plans to prosper you and not to harm you, plans to give you hope and a future."*

He also promises to strengthen those who hope in Him because Isaiah 40:31 says:

> . . . *but those who hope in the* LORD *will renew their strength. They will soar on wings like eagles; they will run and not grow weary, they will walk and not be faint.*

God wants us to have hope. He wants us to hope in Him. But how do we do that? What do we do with the feelings of disappointment from the past? How do we handle the feelings that God let us down?

15

FREE YOURSELF FROM TRAPPED THINKING: GOD LET YOU DOWN!

*No one whose hope is in you
will ever be put to shame.*
—PSALM 25:3

*Many are the plans in a man's heart,
but it is the LORD's purpose that prevails.*
—PROVERBS 19:21

When you have been disappointed, it sure feels like God has let you down. And when you are disappointed again, it feels like God has let you down—again. We can become preoccupied with thinking that God always lets us down when we feel as though we're constantly being disappointed. So, let's take a look at a biblical example of what to do when we feel that we have been disappointed by God and apply these principles to gain freedom from trapped thinking.

There were two single ladies who experienced disappointment because they believed God had let them down; and they clearly communicated their feelings to God, *in person,* about His failure to meet their needs. The women are Martha and Mary, and their relationship with the Lord is recorded in detail in the Scriptures. Martha owned a home in Bethany (Luke 10:38; John 11:1), and she lived there with her sister Mary and brother Lazarus. They were close friends of Jesus, and many times when He was in the area, He would stop by to visit. In John 11, we discover that Lazarus became quite ill, and the sisters sent word to Jesus to come quickly to heal their brother (John 11:3). It is evident that the sisters knew that they could rely on the love Jesus had for them because their message for Jesus included the words, "Lord, the one you love is sick." They were confident that Jesus loved them, they knew that He could heal their brother, and they clearly communicated their desires to Him.

Now the story gets interesting. Jesus received word that Lazarus was ill, but He did not hurry to heal His friend. In fact, the Bible makes it clear that Jesus stayed where He was another two days (John 11:6). Jesus knew Martha and Mary needed Him, yet He purposefully waited until Lazarus was dead before He made His way back to Bethany (John 11:11–14). What a strange reaction for a friend to have. Generally, when a friend is ill, we rush to his side to see what we can do to ease his pain. But Jesus did not do this.

What do you suppose went through Martha and Mary's mind while they were waiting for Jesus? In the beginning, surely they were full of hope. They had a loving and close relationship with Jesus, they knew He was relatively close by, and they knew He could help them. But as the hours and days passed and they watched Lazarus suffer, Martha and Mary must have felt frustration, betrayal, anger, and hurt which intensified the longer Jesus stayed away. But still, there was the glimmer of hope that Jesus would come in time to heal their brother. When Lazarus died, Martha and Mary's hope died with him. So what was Jesus doing while Lazarus was dying? Jesus was *waiting* for him to die and be buried (John 11:11–14). By the time Jesus arrived in Bethany, Lazarus had been buried for four days (John 11:17).

Martha, Mary, and Lazarus were also a popular and well-liked family. The Scriptures tell us that they lived less than two miles from Jerusalem (John 11:18), and many people came to their home to comfort the sisters after the death of their brother (John 11:19). When Martha and Mary heard that Jesus was approaching, only Martha ran out to meet Him; Mary chose to stay in the house (John 11:20). It is easy to relate to Mary's feelings. It seems as if her actions are communicating, "I needed You a week ago when my brother was sick. He is dead now. Why are You showing up now . . . after the fact?" Mary, of the two sisters, was most likely more disappointed in Jesus' late arrival because there is the impression that Mary was closer to Jesus than Martha. It was Mary who sat at His feet listening to every word

(Luke 10:39), not Martha. So it is significant that she did not leave the house to greet Him until He specifically called for her (John 11:28).

Martha's first words when she saw Jesus were, "If you had been here, my brother would not have died" (John 11:21). When Mary came to Jesus, we read the following account in John 11:29–33:

> When Mary heard this, she got up quickly and went to him. Now Jesus had not yet entered the village, but was still at the place where Martha had met him. When the Jews who had been with Mary in the house, comforting her, noticed how quickly she got up and went out, they followed her, supposing she was going to the tomb to mourn there. When Mary reached the place where Jesus was and saw him, she fell at his feet and said, "Lord, if you had been here, my brother would not have died." When Jesus saw her weeping, and the Jews who had come along with her also weeping, he was deeply moved in spirit and troubled.

At this point we see that Jesus cried—touched by the emotions of those around Him (John 11:35), and He raised Lazarus from the dead (John 11:38–45). By looking closely at this account, we can see some principles that can be applied in our own lives when we believe that God has let us down.

REPOSITIONED FOR HIS PURPOSE

When we believe God let us down, what we are doing is attributing human motivations to God. If we are disappointed by someone purposefully, it's usually because that person is mean-spirited and uncaring. When God lets us down, we attribute these negative human qualities to Him; we feel He is mean-spirited or uncaring. Because God is all-powerful and all-knowing, we may conclude that His letting us down is intentional. However, when we believe that God has let us down, we need to understand that we do not know the mind of God. In fact, there is no way that we can know the mind of God, or know what motivates Him, without something that reveals His nature to us. The Bible is a record of God revealing different aspects of Himself to man; because without His revelation of Himself, we have no way of comprehending Him (Job 36:26) or His thoughts and motivations. God clearly tells us that His thoughts and ways are different from ours in Isaiah 55:8–9:

> *"For my thoughts are not your thoughts, neither are your ways my ways," declares the* LORD. *"As the heavens are higher than the earth, so are my ways higher than your ways and my thoughts than your thoughts."*

The good news is that God desires to be known by us. Yes, it is true that we can't fathom or comprehend God, His actions, or lack of action. However, His desire for us to know Him is part of the reason why Jesus came to earth. Not only did Jesus redeem (buy back) mankind (see Appendix), but He also revealed God and His true nature to us (John 14:9–10).

In our biblical example, Martha and Mary could not understand why Jesus would not come and heal their brother. His inaction was unfathomable to them. Yet Jesus had a purpose for not coming. He knew *before* Lazarus died that He was going to raise him from the dead (John 11:11). However, it wasn't until after Lazarus died that Jesus revealed His true purpose to Martha and Mary: to demonstrate to all that in Him is life and the power of resurrection from the dead (John 11:23).

Allow God to reveal the purpose of your disappointment to your heart. If God seemed to have "let you down," it's for a very specific reason. Your disappointment is not because He is careless, thoughtless, mean-spirited, or uncaring. What you might mislabel as God letting you down is actually God guiding you into His purpose.

God is not random; He's very purposeful (Psalm 33:11). He doesn't just randomly remove people from our lives, change our direction, or stick us in new surroundings. God is positioning us to fulfill His purpose. But being "repositioned" sometimes hurts. We become disappointed when our dreams don't work out. We have our own plans, and our lives take plenty of turns, but it is God's purpose that prevails (Proverbs 19:21). To escape from the trapped thinking that God has let you down, the first important step is to realize that God is repositioning you for His purpose. And His ultimate goal is for you to *know* Him, to live out your purpose on earth, and to have eternal life.

GOD IS MOVED BY OUR TEARS

The second principle to help you escape the trap of thinking that God let you down is to know that your feelings do matter to Him. When we believe that God has let us down, it can feel as though our emotions, our tears, don't "touch" Him. But they do. God is touched by our emotions and feelings. We see that Jesus was moved when Mary fell at his feet weeping over the death of her brother. Jesus cried with her. The Bible also gives other examples of God responding to prayer because of tears (2 Kings 20:5; Luke 7:11–15).

Even though God is touched by our tears, it is important to know that He is not manipulated by tears. Just like a mother can watch a child cry when trying to get their way by shedding tears, God too can recognize manipulation. He will not answer prayer just because tears are present. Just like our parents disciplined us for our good despite our many tears, the same is true with God, our heavenly Father. But through it all, God is not insensitive to our feelings. The Bible relates that God lists our tears on a scroll for His record (Psalm 56:8). Tears are also compared to seeds that are planted to get a harvest, for the Word says, "Those who sow in tears will reap with songs of joy" (Psalm 126:5). If you let Him, God stands by to comfort you while He repositions you, because He is concerned with your emotions.

A HOPE AND A FUTURE

The last principle to remember when disappointed is that God is the giver of life (John 11:25), and only He can bring dead things back to life. Part of trapped thinking is seeing only the death of the dream and experiencing the disappointment. We miss the possibilities and opportunities that come into our lives once God has repositioned us. After Lazarus died, all Martha and Mary had was their brother's dead body and a tomb to visit. It never occurred to them that they were being set up by God to participate in one of His greatest miracles—raising Lazarus from the dead.

God wants to resurrect something in you. As we discovered earlier, disappointment is a form of mourning because something has died. However, disappointment kills three things that are critical to a victorious life. God wants to resurrect these things in your life and bring you into victorious living. He wants to raise from the dead your *faith, hope,* and *love.*

Faith

What is faith? Simply stated, *faith* is having trust or confidence in someone or something. In this case, God wants you to trust and have confidence in Him. If the truth be told, we want to put our trust and confidence in ourselves, in money, in a man, in our friends, in virtually anything else but in God. Because if we truly trusted God, we would have already looked past our circumstances to see that He is in control. We wouldn't be locked into the thought of God letting us down, if we truly trusted Him. Although we might not like where He is guiding us, we would still trust His good intentions toward us and, by faith, we would follow Him.

Have you ever felt that you have no faith left? Well, the truth is you do have faith. The Bible says that God has already given us "the measure" of faith (Romans 12:3). God has already given each of us the necessary portion of faith that we need; it may be lying dormant from lack of use, but our faith is still there. When God gives us gifts— like faith—He doesn't take them back (Romans 11:29), but they may "shrink" from lack of use. If you stopped using one of your arms, the muscles would atrophy—stiffen and shrink—from lack of use. You would have to begin to massage and exercise your arm for it to become flexible and strong. The same is true of faith. You need to exercise your faith for it to become flexible and to massage your faith with the Word of God so that it will become strong. Romans 10:17 says:

> So then faith comes by hearing, and hearing by the word of God. (NKJV)

You must hear the Word of God for your faith to grow. To hear the Word, you need to go to a sound Bible-teaching church where you can grow spiritually, and you need to take the time to read your Bible. If you have difficulty understanding your Bible, there are many translations that are easy to understand. Invest in an easy-to-read translation like the *New International Version* or the *New American Standard Bible.*

Hope

Along with faith, God wants to bring *hope* back to life in you. He wants to give you new dreams and goals. He wants you to see the possibilities in your life. God has given each of us gifts, talents, and interests that He wants us to develop and explore. God wants us *in the game,* not seated on the sidelines filled with disappointment or surrounded by broken dreams. As we mentioned in the last chapter, hope brings life. If necessary, reread that section to refresh your memory about the benefits of hope. God wants you to live a full, exciting, and rewarding life. You can only do that with hope living inside of you.

Love

Lastly, God wants to resurrect *love* in your life. Disappointment causes our hearts to "shrink," and we close ourselves off from relationships. For example:

- We're less willing to let new people into our lives.
- We hold ourselves back, and we don't share with others who we are.
- We expect relationships to end in failure.

This is not only true in dating relationships, but also in friendships with people of the same or opposite sex. Not only do we close ourselves off from people, but we close ourselves off from God. God wants to resurrect love in our lives because He wants to resurrect Himself in us. The Word says that *God is love* (1 John 4:8). We cannot truly love until God and His love are birthed in us (1 John 4:7–13).

Let God bring to life that which has died inside of you. Allow Him to resurrect the faith that has died, resuscitate the hope that has passed away, and restore the love that has departed. This is His will for your life for this season—He wants to make you fully alive. For His Word says:

And now these three remain: faith, hope and love. But the greatest of these is love.

(1 Corinthians 13:13)

STRATEGY FOR PEACE

Review the sample prayer below. Use it as a guide to get rid of any disappointment you may be carrying. Then memorize Proverbs 23:18. As you say it aloud, make it personal by substituting the word *my* for *you*.

Lord in Heaven,

I am speaking to You from my heart and I pray to You in the name of Jesus. I confess that I am used to feeling disappointment and I sometimes forget what hope is like. There are times that I have felt that You have let me down. I have felt this way because (<u>name specific reasons why</u>). But You are greater than my heart because You already know my feelings (1 John 3). So right now, I surrender these feelings to You.

Lord God, I look to You to release me from the trap of disappointment (Psalm 25:15). Open my eyes to the possibilities and opportunities that are now in my life because I have been repositioned. Help me to dream new dreams. I thank You that You are resurrecting new life in me.

In Jesus' name.
Amen.

MEMORY VERSE

There is surely a future hope for you,
and your hope will not be cut off.
(Proverbs 23:18)

16

HEALING
YOUR HEART

The crucible for silver and the furnace for gold,
but the LORD tests the heart.
—PROVERBS 17:3

Endure hardship with us
like a good soldier of Christ Jesus.
—2 TIMOTHY 2:3

THE PATH TO HEALING

Let's explore the winding pathway that leads to healing after disappointment. Disappointment is an emotional wound that takes time to heal. But during recovery, self-examination is critical to the healing process. As we discussed in the last chapter, when God repositions us it can be painful. Therefore, trite or glib answers about recovering from disappointment are useless because healing takes not only time, but requires a change in perspective. To heal a heart wounded by disappointment, one must first understand the purpose of disappointment. By discovering the purpose of disappointment, the steps of healing can be found. The three goals of disappointment are:

1. to help you examine yourself,
2. to strengthen you, and
3. to give you a testimony.

Let's take a closer look at each goal.

TO HELP YOU EXAMINE YOURSELF

On the path that leads to healing after disappointment, the first leg of the journey is to examine yourself. There are precious nuggets of gold scattered along the healing pathway—if you're looking for them. These nuggets are called wisdom. We are to learn a lesson from each disappointment. Therefore, it is wise to always ask yourself a series of questions. But even beyond asking yourself the questions, you must give yourself honest answers. God wants us to examine ourselves intently. Lamentations 3:25–29 says:

> The LORD is good to those whose hope is in him, to the one who seeks him; it is good to wait quietly for the salvation of the LORD. It is good for a man to bear the yoke while he is young. Let him sit alone in silence, for the LORD has laid it on him. Let him bury his face in the dust—there may yet be hope.

It is a good thing to sit alone in silence—just you and the Lord. When we "bury our face in the dust," it is figuratively saying that we examine ourselves with a sense of seriousness and focus. Why? So that after our time of self-examination, "there may yet be hope." Hope that we will know ourselves better, that we may see the goodness of God in our situation, that we will change our behavior or the way we think about our situation. God's purpose for self-examination is to bring hope—for Him to breathe His life into your life.

An intricate part of the self-examination process is asking yourself questions and giving yourself very specific and honest answers. The types of questions that are helpful to ask include:

- Why am I disappointed?
- What were my expectations?
- Why did I willingly compromise?
- How did I contribute to this situation?
- How was I weak in this situation?
- How was I strong?
- What behavior did I display that I don't like in myself?

- What would I do differently in this situation?
- What choices did I make?
- Did I fail to make a choice at all and by default allow someone else to make choices for my life?
- What lessons have I learned?
- Is there sin I need to confess?

By answering these questions and others that you make up on your own, you will be able to glean insight into yourself, your motives, and your behavior. But more importantly, it's up to you to learn something new that you can apply to your life in the future.

TO STRENGTHEN YOU

The second purpose of disappointment is to give you strength. God uses disappointment as a tool to make us strong and to give us endurance. In order for us to fulfill our assignment on this earth, God needs for us to be strong, to have endurance, and to have the ability to stand in the face of adversity.

God is raising up soldiers (2 Timothy 2:3) for His army. Like those enlisted in the marines, army, or navy, in God's army we, too, need to be strong, to have endurance and guts. Can you imagine a group of Navy Seals away on a commando mission sniveling because things didn't go their way? It's difficult to imagine because the Seals have a reputation of being tough, smart, and able to get the job done. It's the same with God's army. He doesn't want us to be weak, whiney, and crybaby soldiers; He wants us to have courage and endurance. We learn to have these qualities by getting back up when life knocks us down.

Life is a tough ongoing battle. The ability to look to God to heal your heart after disappointment will enable you to gain the necessary strength and endurance you will need to be victorious. In contrast, there is an attitude that will forever keep us weak and prevent us from becoming emotionally strong: blaming others.

Blame
Blame is easy. We blame others when we do not want to take responsibility for something. However, an important component of

healing involves accepting full responsibility for our actions and for where we are in life. Without the empowerment of responsibility, we are perpetually trapped in the world of being a "victim." When we use the term "victim," we are not talking about one who is an innocent bystander who was injured in a random occurrence (like being hit by a drunk driver), nor are we talking about someone subjected to criminal behavior resulting in injury or death. What we are saying is that we can take on the role of a victim when we don't accept responsibility for our own actions.

Blame is easier for us to stomach because it does not require that we look at how we may have played a role in our own disappointment. It's always easier to believe that it was "someone else's fault" that we are in our present situation. However, blame does two things that are not helpful in our healing:

- *Blame Clouds the Truth.* It's much harder to acknowledge and change our behavior when we do not see that we contributed to our situation.
- *Blame Makes Us Powerless to Change.* If we never examine ourselves, then we do not have the power or inclination to make positive changes in our lives.

We must "own" our mistakes. When we acknowledge our role, choice, mistake, or sin, we can learn to make better choices for our future.

TO GIVE YOU A TESTIMONY

The third purpose of disappointment is to give you a testimony. God wants you as a witness. He wants you to see and experience His goodness toward you, and He wants you to share what you've discovered about Him. As the old saying says, "There is no testimony without a test." Disappointment is a time of testing. The test is: Will you choose to believe God and what He says about you, or will you choose to be swayed by the circumstances? Remember, the purpose of the test is to see your heart.

God allows things to happen to us to see if we will believe in Him and be obedient to Him (2 Corinthians 2:9). Each time the test comes, we have to make the same choice: Am I going to believe God, right now, in my time of pain? Believing God is not a one-time choice, but life asks us that same question over and over again using different circumstances. You have to choose. Either we choose to believe that God has abandoned us, or we can look for the golden nuggets of wisdom amongst the rubble of our disappointment. We pass the test by choosing to believe God and looking for His wisdom. We make the choice of believing God when we:

1. trust Him knowing that He allowed disappointment in our lives now for our ultimate good later.
2. believe that He will turn our disappointment into an opportunity that will allow us to testify of His goodness.

God blesses those who endure and persevere in the face of disappointment. In James 5:11, the Bible says:

As you know, we consider blessed those who have persevered. You have heard of Job's perseverance and have seen what the Lord finally brought about. The Lord is full of compassion and mercy.

Job (pronounced *Jobe*) is used as an example because he was a wealthy man who experienced extreme hardship with the loss of all his children (seven sons and three daughters), his livestock, his home, and his servants—all in one day. Then he contracted painful boils that covered him from head to foot. But Job trusted God and persevered through his test, and the Lord gave Job a testimony that is spoken of today. The Lord blessed Job with twice as much wealth as he had before (Job 42:10–12). God also blessed him by giving him children again—seven sons and three daughters who were the most beautiful women in the land (Job 42:13–15).

God wants you to be a witness to His goodness. He wants to give you a testimony. Then you can be a living witness here on earth to tell others what the Lord has done for you. Disappointment is only a stepping stone to the greater purpose that God has for you. By persevering in this life, not only will you be rewarded on this earth if you persevere; you will also be rewarded once you get to heaven. James 1:12 says:

Blessed is the man who perseveres under trial, because when he has stood the test, he will receive the crown of life that God has promised to those who love him.

17

BABY, PLEASE LOVE ME: DISCOURAGEMENT FROM MISPLACED AFFECTION

Hungry people make poor shoppers.
—UNNAMED THERAPIST

HOT CHOCOLATE

Jake was so fine! Everything about him appealed to her. He was 6´5˝ with coal black eyes, broad, muscled shoulders, a voice smooth like velvet, and had the pantherlike moves of an athlete. He was like a cup of steamy hot chocolate on an icy day. But what Jocelyn liked most was that he wasn't the usual pretty boy-toy, all brawn and no brains; Jake was brilliant and articulate. When they met three years ago, Jake was starting a business featuring his line of clothing for tall men. Now investors are talking to him about taking the company public.

They first met when Jocelyn's cousin asked for help with her daughter's thirteenth birthday party. Jake's daughter, Tiffany, was one of the party guests. She will never forget when she first saw him on that hot mid-July afternoon when he came to pick up Tiffany. Jocelyn was cutting the birthday cake when Jake swung open the gate to the backyard. It was as if time stopped when their eyes locked. Without hesitation he walked up to her, smiled, and said, "I sure would like some cake." That's when it all started.

Their relationship began gradually; maybe once every other week they would go for walks, have a quiet dinner, or take in a movie. During those precious times, Jake shared with Jocelyn his dreams and ambitions. He told her about his divorce four years earlier along with the financial and emotional difficulties that accompanied it. He talked about getting to know himself and how he wasn't ready for a relationship yet. But Jocelyn knew that she could spend the rest of her life with Jake—so she would remind herself not to put pressure on him, but in the meantime, she started praying for God to put her on his heart.

The nature of their relationship took a romantic turn one windy night in November when Jake dropped by. He was discouraged; the business wasn't going well. Jocelyn cooked a delicious dinner, encouraged and prayed for him. At the front door, Jake acknowledged how good she was for him and kissed her for the first time.

Now it's three years later. Jocelyn and Jake have had many such evenings but the relationship is stuck. She has invested a great deal of time and emotional energy on Jake, but he is no closer to committing to her than he was three years ago. It was always something: first, Tiffany wasn't doing well in school and needed his attention; then his business was mentioned on a popular morning talk show and the sales skyrocketed; now he's hiring a staff which, of course, takes his prime time and energy.

Jocelyn is discouraged. She wonders if they will ever get married. Whenever Jocelyn brings up commitment, he always says that now is not a good time. Jocelyn has broken off her relationship with Jake at least six times that she can remember. But they always drift back to each other. Even though he's always so happy to see her, he just doesn't want to commit. Jocelyn is forty-two and she wants to be married. Jake's says that his business is his main priority and spending quality time with his daughter comes next. But he's always quick to add that if he were ready for marriage, he would marry Jocelyn. Her feelings are hurt, and she is stuck in a go-nowhere relationship.

THE PROBLEM OF BEING STUCK

One of the most common causes of discouragement comes from being stuck in a one-way or dead-end relationship. A surprising number of attractive, talented, and lovable women have locked themselves in relationships with men who are either:

- *Unavailable*—he's physically, emotionally, or psychologically distant due to a variety of reasons.
- *Unattainable*—he's not interested or he doesn't even know she exists.
- *Unconscious*—he is so focused on himself or his circumstances that he's unaware of the woman's feelings.

When a man is unwilling to commit, a woman is stuck. She is emotionally depositing her love, energy, and time into someone who is ultimately not a good investment. There are four general types of men that single women need to avoid if they are interested in not misplacing their affection. They are "Mr. Mañana," "The Ball of Confusion," the "Passive Guy," and the "Fantasy Man." None of these men represent "bad" people. They are just ordinary guys that women fall in love with and end up becoming stuck in treadmill relationships with. Although we only describe four categories of men, the reality is that "dead-end" men may possess a number of blended similarities from any of the categories.

MR. MAÑANA

This man's name comes from the Spanish word *mañana*, which means "tomorrow." He puts off making a serious relational commitment to the woman who loves him until a "better time" comes along. If she can just hang in there . . . what she wants or needs from him is just around the corner. You can be sure that with Mr. Mañana, there is always something that will keep him from committing to you today. It is either he's recovering from a previous relationship, he's finishing up his degree, he has something going on with his parents, the company he's working for just got purchased, his son is about to graduate from junior high, he has to sell some property in another state,

119

or he has to wait for the settlement from his 1990 car accident. It doesn't matter what it is—**he just can't commit to you today.**

This man is particularly dangerous because he fosters hope. He puts enough bait on the hook to keep the woman interested, and slowly, very slowly, he reels her in knowing that she will bite every time. Is he doing this on purpose? Maybe, but then again, maybe not. He could genuinely believe that those things need to take place. The situation any woman faces when entangled with Mr. Mañana is not how to get him to commit to the relationship, but rather what would it take for the woman to commit to herself and her future without him. Where is the line that he will cross which clearly indicates when he said "maybe tomorrow" one too many times? The problem in this type of dead-end relationship is not him—it's her.

THE BALL OF CONFUSION

This man is on emotional overload. There is so much going on in his life that he is barely existing—much less being marriage material for someone. Generally, he is just getting over an emotional catastrophe, making a life change, trying to "find himself," or he is in a codependent relationship with someone. For example, he may be:

- newly divorced or widowed after many years of marriage
- dealing with an ill parent
- freshly laid off
- trying to break into a difficult field of work
- helping an ex–drug addicted brother get back on his feet
- finally free of an unhealthy long-term relationship

Whatever his circumstance, the bottom line is he is "trying to get his head on straight."

If he has said the words, "I am not ready for a relationship," or words similar to those—believe him! Generally speaking, his actions are lining up with his words. He "forgets" to call. Unless you initiate contact, you don't hear from him for days, maybe weeks. Frequently, when you get together, it is at your suggestion. His actions matter because he's sending you signals that you must be astute enough to catch. The fact that he remains in your presence is not enough. Is he emotionally giving you what you want, need, and deserve? If not, and he is in the midst of some type of upheaval, you may be in a dead-end relationship with The Ball.

PASSIVE GUY

This man truly lives up to his name. He is passive. To be passive means:

tending not to participate actively; to be inert; to be acted on or affected by some external force rather than causing action; to endure or submit without resistance, to be existing without being active, open or direct.[1]

Are you discouraged because your man is "just along for the ride"? He is not leading, but he's not exactly following either. He's just there—sitting on your couch. You may desire a committed dating relationship with him, but he hasn't made any "moves." You're discouraged because you would like your "friendship" to move forward, but the reality is that you're stuck.

Many women become trapped in relationship limbo with the Passive Guy because neither has clearly communicated the direction of the relationship. Instead, assumptions are made, particularly by the woman, that one day he'll want to commit to her. So the woman ends up waiting, sometimes years, for him to do something. If significant time has gone by and nothing has occurred and her feelings for him are still strong, discouragement sets in.

FANTASY MAN

The difference between the Fantasy Man and all the other men described is that the Fantasy Man is an illusion. In some cases, there is no actual relationship—or if there is one, it's very casual. The reality is the Fantasy Man is not seen as he really is. Instead, he is shrouded by the desires of the woman. The best way to describe the Fantasy Man is to illustrate him using three different examples:

- **The Ultimate Dream Man**—Usually, the way a woman was first attracted to her Ultimate Dream Man was because of his physical attractiveness. Most often he's a movie star, like Denzel Washington, or a fashion model, like Tyson, or an athlete, or some other personality. Many times the woman embellishes the image by attributing emotional characteristics that are not based on any actual experience with the real person. The problem with the Ultimate Dream Man is that if Mr. Nice-Man-Who-is-Real doesn't measure up physically with the Ultimate Dream Man, then he's overlooked. The woman may say, "Oh, he's too nice" or "He's boring." Compared to a jet-setting movie star, of course he's boring. He's leading a normal life. Many a woman has missed her "blessing" because of her grasp on her Ultimate Dream Man.

- **The Man He Could Be**—At least this illusion has some basis in reality because the woman has some sort of relationship with a man in whom she sees tremendous potential—if only he would live up to it. For example, Darla always believed that Tommy could be a tremendous man of God. But Tommy doesn't go to church regularly and barely reads his Bible. But Darla is convinced about Tommy's potential. Sure he has potential. The question is, what is he doing of his own free will with his potential?

  There are three problems with becoming stuck with The Man He Could Be. The first is that the woman is not accepting who this man is *right now*. Part of truly loving someone is receiving who he is—just as he is. This is not to say that a woman can't encourage a man to improve, but his desire to improve *must already be evident by his self-directed corresponding actions*. The second problem is that the man may resent feeling controlled and pushed. There's nothing worse than being pushed to do something you haven't yet decided to do. This pushing doesn't feel like encouragement. To a man, it feels more like tearing down because the woman's "encouragement" is saying that he is inadequate in his present state. The third difficulty involves the woman's hope—for hope springs eternal. His potential is always present; therefore there is the possibility that he will change. Unfortunately, more women become stuck in a dead-end relationship with his potential. This results in becoming discouraged because The Man He Could Be, he isn't—at least right now.

• **The Claimed Man**—Like the Ultimate Dream Man, the woman is initially drawn by his physical attractiveness, yet there is another powerful component: she believes that God has told her that he is her husband. This phenomenon is very prevalent in the church today. We have known women who wasted precious years of their life focused on The Claimed Man. Usually, this is not a momentary experience—women have "stood" for men they have believed to be their husband for *years*. Some women have claimed men who may not know them, but because they have observed them from afar, they feel as if they know them.

When friends of a woman try to tell her that maybe she should reconsider her stance about this man, generally she ignores the advice by chalking it up to their "unbelief." Sometimes, if the friend is persistent, the woman breaks off their friendship because she is being "unsupportive."

If a woman believes God has told her that a particular man is her husband, then the best thing for her to do is to surrender it back to God and let Him work it out. After all, God is all-powerful, and He doesn't need her help. It is critical for her to continue on with her life and not focus on this man. If God works it out, then this is confirmation that she did hear from Him. If the relationship never pans out, she has lost nothing.

The Fantasy Man is just that—a dream or an illusion; he's not real. This man is a trap of the imagination. Women have complained about how their lives are "on hold" until the Fantasy Man comes to his senses and acknowledges their destiny together, or until he lives up to his potential. The problem is not the Fantasy Man; nor is the problem God not answering prayer. The woman's dead-end or one-way relationship and resulting discouragement is rooted in her misplaced affections for an illusion. Are you stuck in a dead-end relationship? Take the following test and see.

QUIZ: ARE YOU STUCK?

Instructions: Take this easy quiz by asking yourself the following questions. In the response, write down the number of the answer that best describes **what you have experienced** most of the time in your relationship.

I Always   2 Very Often   3 Often   4 Sometimes
5 Seldom   6 Very Seldom   7 Never

1. Without any promptings from you, he is the first to initiate the majority of dates, phone calls, and outings with you.

2. He gives emotionally more to the relationship than you do.

3. He expresses to you his desire for the two of you to have a deeper level of commitment.

4. He states his confidence that you are the only woman for him.

5. He talks about desiring to marry you with enthusiasm and anticipation.

6. He is concerned about your emotional well-being and takes the necessary steps to meet your needs.

7. He eagerly takes you around important people in his life (e.g., his parents, close friends, his children).

8. He includes you in his important life decisions.

9. His actions *and* his words show his deep appreciation of your commitment to him.

10. He spends his prime time with you because your relationship is a priority.

Scoring: Add the numbers for each of your responses to find out your *"Are You Stuck?"* score.

10–30 Points
You are not stuck in a go-nowhere relationship. The relationship you're in has the potential to be wholesome and satisfying. This man may be a candidate for marriage. Keep observing his behavior and give the relationship time. Pay attention to areas that had a point score above a "3."

31–50 Points
You have the potential to become stuck in the relationship you are in. You must look closely at the relationship in front of you and determine whether your needs are being met. There are some red flags that you need to evaluate. Also, look at the questions that you scored higher than a "3." Keep your options open. Learn how to establish better boundaries and sharpen your communications skills, especially in the area of relational expectations.

51–70 Points
You are stuck in an unhealthy relationship that has the potential of wasting your valuable time, eating up your emotional resources, and if you're not careful, possibly resulting in financial damage as well. It sounds as if you do not have good boundaries and you may have difficulty saying "no" and meaning it. You need a healthy support system immediately. The good thing is that you took this test and honestly answered the questions. Apply all of the steps recommended and get free from discouragement and from this dead-end relationship.

CHAPTER
18

FREE YOURSELF FROM TRAPPED THINKING: GOD WILL MAKE HIM LOVE ME

*Each man should give
what he has decided in his heart to give,
not reluctantly or under compulsion,
for God loves a cheerful giver.*
—2 CORINTHIANS 9:7

GOD, PLEASE CHANGE HIS HEART

It is common for Christians to want to trust God for what they desire. In fact, God encourages His children to make all our requests known to Him (Philippians 4:6). However, many women become frustrated when they attempt to apply this principle to their desire for a mate. For example, many women have become stuck waiting for God to change the heart of a man they desire to marry. This could be true of the man with whom they are in a dead-end relationship or a man they have "claimed" will be their husband.

The belief is that if a woman loves a man and prays long and hard enough, God will make the man love and commit to her. Women have prayed for years to have God convince a special someone that she will be his wife. They have fasted, begged, pleaded, cried, and waited for God to change the heart of a man they have desired. However, frustration mounts as a woman waits for "God to do His part."

She may feel that she has done everything within her power; therefore, she believes it's up to God to change the heart of the man she passionately desires.

Life can get tricky when we desire something so strongly that we slip into believing that God will force someone to be with us. This is trapped thinking. God will not *force* anyone to romantically love another person or have a dating/marital relationship with them. In fact, God does not force us to love Him or to have a personal relationship with His Son Jesus. When we're asking God to force someone to love us, that person is not given an opportunity to choose to give his love freely. Let's take a look at what it means when each individual freely chooses to give love.

LOVING IS GIVING

When we love someone, we are entering into a relationship of giving. We share our thoughts, our emotions, our intentions, our future, our strengths, and our weaknesses. With love, we are constantly giving ourselves. With that thought in mind, here are some effective ways to think about love relationships. One interesting way to discover how to enter into a relationship is to study what God says about giving. Giving and love work together. Therefore, let's apply the truths of giving to love. By examining the two, we will learn how to free ourselves from trapped thinking. Second Corinthians 9:7 says:

> *Each man should give what he has decided in his heart to give, not reluctantly or under compulsion, for God loves a cheerful giver.*

Using this as our foundational Scripture, let's examine love relationships.

GOD LETS US CHOOSE

"Each man should give what he has decided in his heart to give. . . ."

When it is time to give, God lets each of us choose if we want to give and how much we want to give. *This is the first truth: God lets us choose.* God has given us the right to make decisions—not just about giving, but about every area of our life. He gives us the power to make choices, and He holds us responsible for our decisions. God created us in His image as freewill beings (Genesis 1:27–28). An entity that has a free will is one who is independent to make his or her own decisions—that means we have the power of choice.

God created in us the *capacity* to make choices. Human beings have the ability to think through several different options; we can ponder possible consequences, make a choice, and then take calculated actions to carry out our choice. One of the choices we are allowed to make is whether we want to love someone or not. Therefore, applying our first truth to love, we discover that everyone has the right to choose for themselves *if* they want to love and enter into a loving relationship with another. Keeping this in mind, it is best to allow a man to exercise his freedom of choice when it comes to selecting whom he wants to love. To free yourself from trapped thinking, it's helpful to remember that each person has the right to choose if they want to love, and God respects their choice.

WE CHOOSE HOW MUCH LOVE TO GIVE

". . . what he has decided in his heart to give, not reluctantly or under compulsion. . . ."

The second truth about giving that applies to love is that *God lets us choose how much we want to give.* Not only do we have the right to choose *if* we want to give, but we can determine *how much* we want to give. The same is true in giving love. People must decide for themselves how much of themselves they desire to give. Do they want the relationship to be platonic, a close friendship, romantic, etc.?

You can free yourself from the trap of thinking that God will make him love you by remembering that every person has the right to choose the depth of a relationship. If the relationship has been going nowhere, perhaps a discussion should take place to discover the type of relationship the person wants. Once someone makes that choice, we must respect their wishes. God will not strong-arm a man to move from thinking of a woman as "just a friend" to becoming romantically involved with her. Respect his opinion.

GOD LOVES A CHEERFUL GIVER

". . . for God loves a cheerful giver."

God wants us to give cheerfully. Love is to be freely and cheerfully given. And that can only occur when we have been given the freedom to choose if we want to give our love and how much love we want to give. Then we joyfully give our love because we had the opportunity to choose to give it.

There is also an internal component that occurs inside of us when we are focused on getting a particular man to love us—we begin to lose our joy. We lose our cheerfulness; our satisfaction with life decreases. This is true whether we are in a go-nowhere relationship or we have claimed a certain man.

In closing, these are some things to keep in mind:

- A man is a freewill person created to make his own decisions based on his own desires.
- Claiming a relationship or being in a non-progressing relationship makes us unavailable for blessings that could be around the corner, because we are emotionally fixed on God changing the heart of a particular man.
- God will not force that man to fall in love. Remember that God doesn't force any of us to love Him; nor does He coerce us to love each other. We are allowed to love each other freely.
- God wants to set you free and He desires to restore your joy. He does not want you focused on a particular man. Instead, He wants you alert to the blessings and opportunities He has in store for you.

CHAPTER
19

YOU CAN
BE FREE

It is for freedom that Christ has set us free.
Stand firm, then, and do not let yourselves
be burdened again by a yoke of slavery.
—GALATIANS 5:1

We can be free from discouragement that is a result of misplaced affections. Many times we are in these go-nowhere relationships because we believe this may be our last chance for love or that there will be no one better coming along. That is fear talking. However, if you have a Mr. Go-Nowhere in your life, he is taking up valuable space, time, and resources that could allow a good and healthy relationship to enter into your life. This is true whether you're in an actual relationship with him or if he is "claimed" because you believe he will be your husband. In other words, you don't have space in your life for Mr. Wonderful. Some of us say, "Well, *when and if* Mr. Wonderful does come along, I'll make space for him." It doesn't work like that. Because there is no space, Mr. Wonderful does not come. So how do we make space for the good and get free from discouraging relationships? Here are the steps.

EMPOWER YOURSELF

In situations of misplaced affection, women feel powerless. It feels as though someone else has control of the outcome of our lives. Whether our lives will be happy or sad depends on *someone else's* decision about being in a relationship with us. What we fail to realize is that *we also have the power to choose.* We, too, are freewill human beings that God endowed with the ability to choose—just like men have the ability to choose. But why don't we exercise our God-given right of choice in relationships? Why do we wait on pins and needles for someone to wake up and recognize that we are good in their lives? Why do we waste years of our lives running behind some man who "forgets" to call us? Why are we praying and confessing the name of some man who doesn't know we exist? Why? Because of our perspective.

We believe that he is the prize, not us. We hold him in higher esteem than we hold ourselves. Don't we know that *we* are jewels? We must change our perspective to agree with what God says about us: that we are the prize and the blessing for the man. God said the man who finds a wife has received favor and a blessing from God (Proverbs 18:22). God also likened a good wife to a prize higher than rubies (Proverbs 31:10). Wives are also described as a crown (Proverbs 12:4) for the head of their husbands. Since we are the prize, if someone is not treating us as a prize, or does not recognize us as a gift, then it is time to move forward with our lives to someone who can see our wonderful qualities. So how do you know if someone thinks of you as his prize? By asking questions.

ASK QUESTIONS

In order to make good choices, we need sound information. The way we get information is by asking questions. Sometimes, we're afraid to ask questions because we are afraid to hear the answers. If you're afraid to hear the answer to a question, then that is truly a signal that it is a question that may need to be asked. For example, if a woman has been seeing a man for eight months and she is not sure if they are exclusively dating, then there is a problem. If she desires to be married, then she needs to know where the relationship is going. What are his intentions? What does he think of her? These are all very important questions that she has a right to know the answer to because her time is valuable.

Be wise in asking your questions. Choose a time when the two of you can talk unhurried. Ask questions respectfully and be prepared to answer any questions he may have. No matter how many years may have been "invested" in a relationship, this is not a time to make assumptions. Ask questions, but most importantly, listen to the answers he gives.

LISTEN TO THE ANSWERS

So many women ask good questions but never hear the answers. For example, a woman may ask a man, "What are you looking for in a wife?" If he says, "I don't believe in marriage," or "I don't need a wife because I can take care of myself," HEAR HIS ANSWER! When a man says something like that, he is telling you the truth! He does not want to get married—at least not right now. Woman after woman falls into the trap of thinking that she can change a man by believing that she can make his life so wonderful that he will "have to marry her." NOT TRUE! He has given an honest answer. Respect it. The answer may not be one we want to hear—but listen to it and *don't try to change his mind*. If his answer conflicts with what you want or need in your life, consider it a signal to move on. Keep your ears particularly tuned in for words describing your relationship as a "friendship." There's nothing wrong with friendship as long as that is what you want. But when you are looking for marriage, a platonic friendship is not enough.

CLEAN HOUSE

Don't beg or plead for the man to see what a great woman you are. Instead, move on with your life. And do so sweetly. Don't let his last impression of you be one where there is screaming, shouting, recriminations, and tears. State to him, very nicely, that you have enjoyed the time you have spent together, but you feel as though it is time for you to move forward with your life. Clearly state that your desire is to one day get married to a man who appreciates you and wants you to be the mother of his children. (Resist telling him that you thought he was that man.) For that reason, you need to make space in your life, so you would appreciate it if he not call or come by. Tell him you hope he finds what he is looking for, and wish him the best. Be sincere. Make your speech short and sweet, but you must absolutely mean it. If you cannot do this with resolve—then it is better not to do it at all. Build yourself up further until you know that you can move forward with your life. Seek out family, friends, or a Christian therapist who may help you reach this point.

Don't use the "clean house" step to manipulate a man into making a commitment to you. This is a very powerful step that enables a woman to take control of her life and to exercise her choice. Use this step only if you are serious about desiring to make space for a new and fulfilling relationship. When women use this step as a ploy to wrangle some sort of commitment, they can become trapped in the break-up/make-up cycle in a relationship. It just means that the woman wasn't truly ready to break off the relationship and move forward.

BE PREPARED

When a woman uses the "clean house" step, 90 percent of the time the man attempts to reenter the woman's life. They'll usually wait about two or three weeks to let her cool off, and then they'll call to "test the waters." This phenomenon is very similar to feeding a stray cat. The stray comes around every day because you're feeding it. Even if you stop feeding the cat, it will still come back just in case there is food available. It is the same thing with the Go-Nowhere relationship. He comes back! Be polite yet firm and do not reestablish a relationship with him. Keep the conversation short and don't ask him any questions about his life; simply wish him the best and move forward.

Setting limits, moving on, and being by ourselves takes courage. Oftentimes we have the strong desire to move forward from an unhealthy relationship, but we lack the inner strength to do so. The hunger for companionship often has more control of us than we would like to admit. We all have the need for relationship; that is how God created us. And He created us with a "relationship void," an emptiness that only God Himself can appropriately fill. Many of us often feel that if we completely end the relationship with Mr. Go-Nowhere, the emptiness or the relationship void will become so strong that it will either drive us crazy or into another unhealthy relationship.

We can get rid of that nagging urgency for relationship by filling it with healthy relationships. When we fill our void with healthy relationships, it gives us the courage and strength to make right choices. Start by refreshing your relationship with Jesus Christ. He is the ultimate void-filler and your strength-giver. When we learn to be in intimate relationship with Him, He provides us with the endurance we need to wait for His best. God's desire is for us not only to be connected to Him, but to others as well. Join a church growth group, make new friends, reignite older loving friendships with caring people, reconnect with family, and build yourself a network of trusted companions. It is through solid, healthy relationships with God and others that we gain the strength to close the doors to time-wasting and heartbreaking relations.

MEMORY VERSE

For God did not give us a spirit of timidity,
but a spirit of power, of love and of self-discipline.
(2 Timothy 1:7)

SECTION THREE

BITTERNESS

CHAPTER

20

THE BONDAGE
OF BITTERNESS

*My friends and companions avoid me because of
my wounds; my neighbors stay far away.*
—PSALM 38:11

*But you, O Sovereign LORD, deal well with me for
your name's sake; out of the goodness of your love,
deliver me. For I am poor and needy,
and my heart is wounded within me.*
—PSALM 109:21–22

TWO SISTERS

Nicole's older sister Bailey never seemed to get it together. Even though Bailey was three years older, their mother would always tell Nicole to take care of her. Through the years, Nicole felt she was always either getting Bailey out of a jam or cleaning up one of her messes. But Mama's words would always ring in her ears that they had to watch out for each other. Now that she's dead, it's just the two of them.

Bailey was an actress. This meant she was sometimes in Los Angeles, or in New York, or somewhere in between. Every so often, she would appear at Nicole's door asking to camp out for a couple of weeks. Nicole would give Bailey a little lecture about staying in contact but, of course, she would let her stay. But Bailey never left in two weeks. Usually, her visit would last two or three months, maybe longer. The stays wouldn't be so bad if Bailey contributed financially, but usually she would kick in just a few bucks, never enough to cover the food she ate, the increase of the electricity bill, or the long distance calls. When a gig would come up, Bailey would leave as abruptly as she arrived.

One night when Bailey showed up asking if she could stay, she was clearly agitated. Nicole agreed, as usual. But two days later Bailey disappeared, along with Nicole's notebook computer, her leather coat, a CD player, and $300. Nicole filed a missing persons report with the police. A week later, the police contacted Nicole telling her that Bailey was fine and in Chicago. Bailey finally called Nicole—two weeks later. She didn't apologize for stealing from Nicole but instead lied to her. Fed up, Nicole blew up. She called Bailey a liar and told her she would never forgive her or see her again.

After she hung up, Nicole sat in her darkened living room thinking about Bailey. She was hurt that her sister would steal from her and angry with herself for not seeing through Bailey sooner. Nicole thought about the money she spent providing for Bailey. She remembered all of the times she had helped her sister over the years. That's when Nicole promised herself that she would *never be that stupid again.* She concluded that Bailey was no good and a user. She vowed she would never let Bailey take advantage of her again!

Nicole cleaned up after Bailey one last time. She methodically cleaned out everything Bailey had in her house. Nicole packed away every picture with Bailey in it and all the gifts Bailey had ever given her. When she finished, Nicole showered, dressed, went to the police department, and filed a theft report.

That was five years ago. The calls have slowed down considerably, and quite frankly, Nicole couldn't care less. The first year Bailey pretended as though everything was still the same—she would try to engage her in conversation and joke with her. Nicole's responses were curt, and she would hang up on her as quickly as possible. The second year, Bailey finally apologized by sending a beautiful leather jacket with a note. Nicole read the apology, thought to herself, "Too little, too late," and threw the note away.

A month later a check for $600 came from Bailey with her new telephone number. Again she apologized and asked Nicole to call. Nicole cashed the check and threw the number away. On Nicole's birthday, a flower arrangement arrived from Bailey. Nicole gave it to her next-door neighbor. A fat letter came next from Bailey. On the

140

outside of the letter Nicole read the words "I've changed. Please forgive me." Nicole carried the letter in her purse for a week without reading it. Then she remembered how manipulative Bailey could be and how she had vowed to herself she would never fall for any more of her tricks, so that night she burned Bailey's unopened letter in the kitchen sink.

Year three, a new laptop computer was delivered. Over that year there were four or five voicemail messages and another letter. Year four, Bailey sent her a wedding invitation. Year five, a picture of a cute little baby girl arrived in an unsigned card with no return address. On the back of the picture were written the words . . . "Her name is Nikki. I miss you."

WHAT IS BITTERNESS?

Bitterness is the baggage we carry when we can't get over something someone has done to us. It bubbles up when we have been wronged or when life doesn't go our way. Bitterness is the intense feeling of resentment that arises out of an occurrence that is perceived to be an injustice. Not only is bitterness a feeling, but it is also a process. It is the gradual turning of our once warm hearts cold. The results of bitterness are seen in the withdrawing of love, the turning away from others, the protective walls we build around our hearts, and the unwillingness to trust. It is when we try to shield ourselves from harm that we close ourselves off from love, trust, and interacting with others because we believe that those qualities are what got us in trouble in the first place. We reason that if we didn't trust this person, we would not have been hurt by them.

Nicole's bitterness boiled over when Bailey stole her stuff and then lied about it. But really, the seeds of Nicole's bitterness toward Bailey sprouted back in their childhood. Their mother (rightly or wrongly) put the responsibility to care for Bailey onto Nicole—too heavy a burden for a child to handle. Nicole's resentment of taking care of and cleaning up after Bailey grew over the years. To Nicole, Bailey's last disappearance and theft was representative of their whole relationship. As far as she was concerned, Bailey had been stealing from her all her life. Therefore, even after Bailey replaced the items taken, her apologies went unheeded because those last few items were not as important as the intangibles, such as trust, love, and sisterly care, that were stolen over the years. When Nicole remarked about Bailey's first apology, "Too little, too late," for her that was the truth of the matter. Nicole's heart had turned away from Bailey.

WHAT BITTERNESS LOOKS LIKE

Some say bitter people are realists. They know that everything doesn't always turn out all right and that living happily ever after just doesn't exist. They are the ones who "call it as they see it" because they can smell trouble a mile away and can spot a loser in a minute. But what is the emotional cost? Bitterness extracts an incredibly high penalty in the life of the bitter person. Bitterness keeps us separated, alone, unloving, and unlovable.

Bitterness is the process of our heart turning cold. Sometimes it's hard to gauge the subtle cooling-down process bitter people go through. How can we tell when our hearts are growing colder? What does it look like? When we are bitter on the inside, it shows in how we think, in our actions toward others, and it even manifests itself in our physical body.

RECOGNIZING OUR BITTERNESS

When we are bitter, we have a tendency to be critical. We see what is wrong and we're quick to point it out. We talk about the faults of others—in fact, it's one of our favorite topics of conversation. Also, when we are bitter, we're overly sensitive and snippy. We examine every little thing people do: we check out their tone, their choice of words, even the look in their eye when they converse with us. People try to tell us that we're "overly sensitive," but we dismiss their observations by saying, "That's just who I am."

Bitterness causes us to second-guess people. We read into the actions of others and frequently misinterpret their motives. We have difficulty looking people in the eye, because we don't want to get close to them—and we don't want to be known by them. We are unforgiving of people who make mistakes. We expect more openness from others than we are willing to give them in return.

Also, when we are bitter, we have a hard time controlling our tone of voice when we communicate. The things we say actually come out in a harsher manner than we intend many times. We are sarcastic, cutting, and mean. Sometimes we're so focused on showing our displeasure with a particular person that we come across as spiteful, vindictive, and sour. We want to return tit for tat. We desire to make people "pay" for their actions. We check up on people (we call it doing our "homework"). We constantly complain about others until our friends want to avoid us. When people tell us that we're controlling, we say, "We're taking care of business." We "pull back" in relationships; therefore, people tell us that we're hard to know or that they don't know us. And, as we age, we ultimately end up with very few friends.

Not only does bitterness diminish the quality of our relationships, but it also takes a toll on our bodies. Being bitter is draining. It takes energy to stay hypervigilant. Many times bitter people suffer from high blood pressure, headaches, digestive problems, ulcers, and infections. Our immune system becomes weakened, and we become susceptible to colds. Many times, bitter people struggle with their weight. We eat because it gives us something to do. We eat because it's our only pleasure. We eat because we feel empty and lonely.

So, how did we become bitter? What kind of experiences did this to us? When did this happen?

YOUR OPPORTUNITIES FOR BITTERNESS

Every person on earth has a reason to be bitter. Life is filled with wrongs, insults, slights, injuries, and cruelty. We have all suffered because of someone else's actions. We have experienced their lack of consideration for our personhood. Our feelings have been trampled, our thoughts dismissed, and our physical bodies have been violated.

Bitter experiences can happen at any phase of life. For some of us, bitter experiences happened at birth. We were unwanted, therefore not held; thus we were left to ourselves and unloved. For others, bitter experiences happened at an older age. For each of us, bitterness comes into our lives via a different route.

Listed below are some experiences that can lead to bitterness. How many apply to you?

_____ You have been lied to or deceived in a relationship (dating, friendship, parental, etc.)

_____ Loss of a physical ability, self-sufficiency, or strength

_____ Swindled or tricked out of money

_____ Forced to abort your unborn child

_____ Not believed when telling the truth

_____ Broken engagement or canceled wedding

_____ Loved one assaulted or murdered

_____ Your efforts or love is unappreciated

_____ Neglected as a child

_____ Not dating for extended periods of time or never being asked out

_____ Loss of reputation or good name

_____ Physically beaten during your lifetime

_____ Made to feel foolish or suffer public humiliation

_____ Prolonged loneliness

_____ Laid off from work

_____ Bullied by others in the past or present

_____ Blamed—whether at fault or not

_____ Victim of ruthless/cold treatment

_____ Unplanned pregnancy and becoming a single parent

_____ An injustice has occurred that has not been righted

_____ Prolonged, undiagnosed, or misdiagnosed illness

_____ Someone owes you an apology

_____ Lack of emotional and financial support for child(ren) by their father

_____ Your suffering is ignored by others

_____ Loss of a home

_____ Boyfriend (or husband) left you for another woman (or man)

_____ Passed over for a promotion or transfer

_____ Being the scapegoat or black sheep of a family

_____ Loss of a child through death or custody

_____ Loss of a husband through desertion or death

_____ Having your feelings minimized or discarded

_____ Your secret was told—a loss of privacy

_____ Having to pay the penalty for someone else's wrong

_____ Molested

_____ Raped

_____ Abandoned

These are just some of the things that happen in life that can cause bitterness. As a result of these experiences, we struggle through life with burdens, secrets, and a whole lot of pain. Take time to reflect on each item you have selected. Examine your response to determine if these experiences are a route to bitterness. God wants to set us free from bitterness; He is the burden-lifter, and He is the Healer of our pain. We no longer have to remain captive to the power of bitterness. Let's find out how to break free.

CHAPTER
21

I CAN'T FORGIVE: BITTERNESS AND UNFORGIVENESS

*For I see that you are
full of bitterness and captive to sin.*
—ACTS 8:23

HIT AND RUN

Sheila was a woman on the fast track. At age twenty-eight, she was already an editor at a national advertising firm. Andre was the new director transferred in from their Chicago office. It was well-known throughout the company that Andre had a bright future—he was being groomed to take over his mentor's position as the national vice-president of marketing. Andre was smart, handsome, and quite personable. When they were introduced, the first thing Sheila noticed was that Andre had a way of looking at her and listening to what she said as if she were the only person in the room.

Their relationship didn't just happen overnight. Because they were the only two Blacks in management at the company, a kinship had gradually developed. It started with him asking her opinion about different projects, with an occasional lunch scattered here and there. When they were alone, they had fun and very animated conversations. However, in the corporate setting, one would not know they knew much more than each other's name.

During that year, Andre and Sheila drew closer to each other. Over dinner one lovely April evening, Sheila confessed to him that she had fallen in love. From that very night and for sixteen wildly romantic weeks, they were lovers. Toward the end of July, Sheila discovered she was pregnant. Andre was insistent that she abort; Sheila didn't want to. They went round and round for a couple of weeks until he abruptly broke off the relationship. About a week passed with no contact, and late one afternoon, Sheila went to Andre's office to talk to him.

His back was to her when she walked in, so she didn't realize he was on the phone until she overheard him. Thinking back on it, Sheila has realized that she should have either left right away or made her presence known. If she had, perhaps her life would be different today. Whomever Andre was talking to, he was telling them that he was excited about returning to Chicago and reuniting with his fiancée. Sheila clearly remembers the words, "No, we haven't set a date yet but we will when I get back next month . . . (pause) Remember that little piece of business I told you about? Yeah, that's the one . . . No, she won't get rid of it . . ."

Sheila didn't hear much more because she grabbed what was closest to her hand—his stapler. She threw it hard, and it hit him on the back of his head. The blow stunned him and gave her the advantage. Sheila lunged at him. Overall, the rampage lasted about six minutes before security officers ran in. The computer monitor was smashed, chairs were overturned, the phone line had been yanked out of the wall, and the fax machine was damaged. Andre required fifteen stitches. Within thirty minutes, Sheila was fired. A police report was made. Even though Andre wasn't going to press charges, the D.A. pursued the case. Since that afternoon, Andre hasn't spoken to Sheila. But his lawyer relayed to her that Andre had "graciously" paid for all property damage and instructed her that she was to have no direct contact with him or his fiancée—ever. A friend from the office told Sheila that Andre moved back to Chicago within a week, thirty days earlier than planned. Sheila felt she had no choice but to accept the plea bargain of three years of probation, 120 hours of community service, and court-ordered counseling. That was fifteen months ago.

Sheila is bitter and stuck. She's bitter because she had difficulty finding an employer who wanted to hire a pregnant woman on probation. She wasn't able to find a job until after the baby was born— unfortunately, her current job only pays a little more than half of what she was making before. She's also bitter because she never heard from Andre. He has not spoken to her; nor has he ever apologized for deceiving her. Now she hears he's married and the new national vice-president of marketing. Andre has also made it clear that he doesn't ever want to see his son. His lawyer sent Sheila his waiver of parental rights with the stipulation that they make no attempts to contact him with pictures or letters. Without her asking, Andre provides $600 per month for child care. No address appears on the checks because they are issued from the attorney's corporate account.

Sheila rehashes her past by rehearsing scenarios in her mind and imagining that things could be better today if only she had done something differently. She has lost her joy, not just because she has the responsibility of a baby, but because she is captive to her past. Her relationship with Andre changed her whole life—for the worse. Sheila is crushed that Andre has not spoken to her, and every day she thinks about his silence. She hates Andre for making her feel like a bothersome piece of trash. His silence has made her bitter, and she blames him for ruining her life. Sheila says that she is bitter with good cause. She was used and then tossed aside; she can't forgive Andre, and she won't even try.

DOING HARD TIME

When we are a captive of our past, it is a telltale sign that we are incarcerated in the prison of bitterness. Sheila is a prisoner of her past. She is held hostage by a segment of time in her life in which profound disappointment and disillusionment occurred. There is nothing wrong with feeling disappointed or disillusioned, except when these feelings control our lives and keep us in bondage. Sheila is in bondage. God says in Acts 8:23 that when we are full of bitterness, we are captive to sin.

Bitterness leads us into captivity. It's just like being arrested and being led away to the penitentiary. When we are dealing with bitterness, it's as if we are in a prison doing hard time. According to the *American Heritage Dictionary*, the word *prison* comes from the word *prehendere,* which means to take hold of; arrest; to capture.[1] And that is what happens to us when we have an experience that leads to bitterness—we become a "captive" of that experience. It has "arrested" our attention, our thoughts, and our future. By being unable to forgive those who have wronged us, we automatically become inmates in the prison of bitterness.

Like any other prison, the prison of bitterness is a frightening and lonely place. When people talk about their prison experience in a place like Folsom Prison, Norfolk State Prison, Chino, or even the county jail, three things commonly happen to the people that go there. They often experience:

- isolation,
- a loss of identity, and
- no peace.

Isolation

One of the stated purposes of a prison is to separate the inmate from the rest of society because they pose a threat to the safety of others. When we are imprisoned by bitterness, we experience something similar—except with a twist. Because we have been hurt and are bitter, we isolate ourselves from others because *they* pose a threat to *us.* In the previous chapter, we discussed how bitterness is a process of our hearts growing cold and it keeps us separated, alone, unloving, and unlovable. Not only does bitterness separate us from others, but bitterness isolates us from our "present." Our "here and now." We get stuck in the past where the incident occurred. We replay our experience in our minds over and over again. We become so consumed with our past that we miss our present.

Bitterness also isolates us from God. Our relationship with Him suffers tremendously when we are bitter. In fact, the word *sin* means to be separated from God. When we are dealing with bitterness, we are captive to sin; we are held hostage in a state of separation from God.

Loss of Identity

Bitterness causes us to lose our identity. When an inmate enters a penitentiary, one of the first things he is assigned is a number. That number is on a hospital-like bracelet they must wear on their clothes. They are referred to by their number and not their name. They lose their identity. Bitterness also causes us to lose ourselves. Our dreams and desires are an intricate part of our identity. Bitterness squeezes out our dreams. Bitterness causes us to put our lives on "hold." We have a hard time making forward progress—achieving our dreams and going after our goals.

No Peace

Prison is a violent place and there is nothing pleasant or peaceful about being there. It is a place of sorrow, anger, and loss. Similarly, there is no emotional or spiritual peace when we are trapped in the prison of bitterness. We are in mourning about what could have been while we are angrily trying to accept our new circumstances. We live in-between the imaginary world of "what if" and the reality of "what is." It's the back and forth commute between these two worlds that causes a sort of madness. Others around us can see that we are clearly in pain and emotional distress, but they are at a loss as to how to help us. In our misery, we draw conclusions about the one we can't forgive . . . the one we hold, rightly or wrongly, accountable for our current distress.

THERE IS A WAY OF ESCAPE

Bitterness never wants to set you free. Bitterness wants to fulfill its own purpose—what it was designed to do in your life. The purpose of bitterness is to:

- forever keep you isolated with anger and blame,
- withhold your dreams and desires,
- hinder you from discovering and fulfilling your purpose,
- keep you stuck in the past and missing your present,
- have the wound remain fresh and sensitive,
- prevent you from experiencing peace, and
- keep you captive to sin and separated from God.

But God created a way for us to escape from our bitter experiences. God wants us to have the victory over all bitterness. God realizes that life is full of bitterness, but He does not want you loaded down and burdened by it. God says in Hebrews 12:15:

See to it that no one misses the grace of God and that no bitter root grows up to cause trouble and defile many.

Bitterness is a root which can continuously grow in our lives, if we allow it. By permitting it to grow, God says bitterness will cause you "trouble." But not only that, it will cause us to "miss the grace of God." Included in God's grace is His favor, His active power in us, and His blessings for our lives. God knows that it is our human nature *not* to forgive and we need His strength to help us to forgive.

But you may say, "I can't forgive. You don't know what has happened to me. No one has apologized and I'm the one paying the price for what others did to me. They seem to have gotten away with it, but here I am suffering. I can't let them off the hook. I can't forgive them. And besides that, I have the right to hold this grudge after what was done to me."

22

FREE YOURSELF FROM
TRAPPED THINKING:
I HAVE A RIGHT TO
HOLD THIS GRUDGE

*Do not seek revenge or bear
a grudge against one of your people,
but love your neighbor as yourself. I am the LORD.*
—LEVITICUS 19:18

There are some life experiences that we will not be able to avoid. One of the most common is the pain we experience from being hurt by others. Whether it's by their words or actions, we all will experience personal pain because of the actions of another. Sometimes people deliberately hurt us, and other times, it's unintentional. After being hurt, we either mend our relationship, or we find ourselves in an unresolved situation. When we are hurt, bitter, and angry, we often feel that holding on to a grudge is justified. Little do we know that our apparent "right" to hold our grudge is hurting us more than we realize. When our thoughts perpetuate the idea that we have the right to hold a grudge, we are backing our own lives into a corner. However, a way out is possible—if we start by understanding the implication of our stance and learn exactly what is at stake.

UNFORGIVENESS: THE ULTIMATE BOND-BREAKER

What we call grudge-holding, the Bible describes as unforgiveness. When we are unforgiving toward another, we are actually saying that person owes us something. There is a debt they must pay to us. And if they don't pay up, we withhold various things from them, such as love, caring, openness, conversation, politeness, and friendship. When we commit ourselves to a grudge, the close bond that we have with others is immediately jeopardized. Nothing good comes from a grudge, nor is anything positive produced from unforgiveness. In fact, Satan's secret is that he uses unforgiveness to destroy relationships. Not only does unforgiveness destroy the relationship with the person whom we have a grudge against, but it damages our relationship with others as well. Practicing unforgiveness increases the likelihood that we will continue to be unforgiving to anyone who wrongs us. Each time we *don't* forgive, it gets easier for us to hold a grudge.

Trapped thinking deludes us into believing that *"we'll show them . . ."* if we hold on to a grudge. But that's exactly what Satan wants—our relationships strained by unforgiving attitudes. A decision to be unforgiving only leads to damaged or severed relationship. Therefore, unforgiveness is the ultimate bond-breaker because it separates us from others and from God.

BUILDING OUR MOST IMPORTANT RELATIONSHIPS

We are created to enjoy three types of relationships, all of which are precious to God. They are: the relationship we have with ourselves (Mark 12:31), others (1 Peter 3:8), and our relationship with God (Matthew 22:37). Holding a grudge is a choice. Forgiving is a choice. The grid on the next two pages describes how to develop and maintain the type of relationship you desire.

Type of Relationship	To Maintain a Grudge Relationship	To Maintain a Forgiving Relationship
With Self	Remember how others hurt you and ruminate on every detail of the incident daily.	Whenever you recall what others have done to you, make it an issue of prayer. Pray about it each time it comes to mind.
	Learn to enjoy being bitter and angry. Make it permanent by deciding you will never change or give in.	Ask God to show and help you identify and take responsibility for your part.
	Convince yourself that holding a grudge is getting back at the other person even when it is only making you unhappy with yourself.	Let God know you are willing to change.
With Others	Don't believe that Satan is the real enemy. Instead, grow so bitter toward the other person that you learn to hate them.	Remember that God does not want us to fight with each other. Instead, realize that Satan is the one we should stand against (Ephesians 6:12).
	Harden your heart against all those who have hurt you so that it becomes easier to cut off anyone with whom you have a conflict	Be willing to examine yourself and not let a root of bitterness grow inside your heart.

Type of Relationship	To Maintain a Grudge Relationship	To Maintain a Forgiving Relationship
With Others	Become vindictive, cynical, and sarcastic toward others.	Ask God to help you approach and apologize to anyone He lays on your heart or anyone you may have hurt in the past.
	Never trust anyone again.	Learn new skills to help you enhance your relationships.
		Avoid words and actions that push people away.
With God	Blame God for every broken relationship you have. After all, He could have stopped them from treating you that way whenever He wanted.	Be honest with God. Let Him know exactly how you feel about those who have hurt you and how you feel toward Him. Know that He can handle your pain.
	Never slow down enough to acknowledge that you are angry and bitter with God. Stay busy so that you will never have an idle moment to think about how much He misses you.	Be sure to talk to God regularly about your difficult relationships.

Type of Relationship	To Maintain a Grudge Relationship	To Maintain a Forgiving Relationship
With God	Only focus on how God is not meeting your needs. Never acknowledge the grudge you have against Him.	Unconfessed sin only separates you from God and makes it easy for you to hold. a grudge against Him Therefore, confess your sins regularly so you can maintain a close relationship with God (1 John 1:9).

Holding a grudge only isolates you, but there is a way to move past the hurt. The way of escape from grudge-holding is through forgiveness. But suppose you're not really interested in forgiving. Why should you forgive? And if you were to forgive, how would you do it?

23

UPROOT
UNFORGIVENESS

Be merciful, just as your Father is merciful.
Do not judge, and you will not be judged.
Do not condemn, and you will not be condemned.
Forgive, and you will be forgiven.
Give, and it will be given to you.
A good measure, pressed down, shaken together
and running over, will be poured into your lap.
For with the measure you use, it will be measured to you.
—LUKE 6:36–38

MAKE THE DECISION TO FORGIVE

Forgiveness is a decision. Forgiveness is not a feeling. Forgiveness is not based on the actions of the other person, nor is it based on whether he or she seems properly sorrowful. Forgiveness is the only ticket out of the prison of bitterness. God repeatedly commands us to forgive one another. Jesus even tells a parable (a story or an example which illustrates a moral point) recorded in Matthew 18 which gives a graphic example of the consequences of unforgiveness. The parable is about a wealthy man who was owed a great deal of money (10,000 talents) by his servant. The servant could not pay his employer what was owed, so his wife and children were about to be sold into slavery to pay the debt. But the servant fell to his knees and begged the wealthy man to have mercy on him, and the man "forgave" the debt—meaning the servant's slate was wiped clean so he no longer owed the money. But later on, that same servant went out and found a man who only owed him a little bit of money and he attacked him. When the man begged for mercy, the servant had the man thrown into prison instead. The wealthy man was told of what the forgiven servant had done, and what he said to the servant is recorded in Matthew 18:32–34:

> *"You wicked servant," he said, "I canceled all that debt of yours because you begged me to. Shouldn't you have had mercy on your fellow servant just as I had on you?" In anger his master turned him over to the jailers to be tortured, until he should pay back all he owed.*

In Matthew 18:35, Jesus emphasizes the point of the parable with these words:

> *This is how my heavenly Father will treat each of you unless you forgive your brother from your heart.*

God is represented by the wealthy man, and we are the servant. God has forgiven us of debts that we can never pay. He wipes our slate clean of our sins when we have a relationship with Him. He asks us to do the same with others who sin against us. The parable emphasizes how God views the sins. First, our sin against Him is a great debt, one that we could never pay. And He willingly forgives us our sins when we ask Him. Whatever sin another human being has done to us (no matter what it is) is not comparable to the sin we have already committed against God. Because He has forgiven us our sins against Him, He expects us to forgive others who have sinned against us. God wants us to show mercy to one another, just as He has shown us mercy.

In the story, the wealthy man turned his servant over to the jailers to be tortured. How cruel, you may think. But that's the same thing that happens to us when we don't forgive. We are locked away in the prison of bitterness and tortured emotionally and spiritually. We remain "stuck." Forgiveness is the way out of prison.

Here are two more amazingly clear Scriptures about forgiveness:

> *For if you forgive men when they sin against you, your heavenly Father will also forgive you.*
>
> (Matthew 6:14)

Then Peter came to Jesus and asked, "Lord, how many times shall I forgive my brother when he sins against me? Up to seven times?" Jesus answered, "I tell you, not seven times, but seventy-seven times."
(Matthew 18:21–22)

We are encouraged and commanded to forgive. Therefore, let's be obedient to the Lord and get free from the prison of bitterness.

THE ACT OF FORGIVENESS

As we stated earlier, forgiveness is a decision. It is not a feeling—because we rarely feel like forgiving. Forgiveness is not dependent on a mood, a desire, or an urge. Forgiveness is a life-freeing, burden-lifting choice that you make for yourself and your future.

STRATEGIC MOVES

Here is the route to freedom. Read **all** of the instructions before you start.

Sit down with a sheet of paper and write down who has offended you and why. Keep it simple. For example:

My Forgiveness List
(Today's Date)
I have made the decision to forgive the following people:

- Judy—Stole my watch
- James—Broke my heart
- Justin—Doesn't support his child
- Daddy—What he did to Mama
- That man who rear-ended my car last month while talking on his cell phone
- Tina—The girl who always teased me in junior high school

161

Take a moment to pray about each situation. You can pray something like this:

Dear heavenly Father:

You know that I don't feel like forgiving (<u>put in the person's name</u>), but I have made the decision this day to forgive him/her. You know what he/she/they did to me (<u>summarize the situation or event</u>). But You said in the Bible that if I forgive, I will be forgiven. I desire to be set free from bitterness. I confess that my heart has been hardened because of this experience, but I ask You to heal my heart. Therefore, as an act of faith, I choose to forgive (<u>put their name in</u>) this day.

In Jesus' name.

Take your time. Repeat this step until you finish your list of people.

For some people, after they finish praying about the people and situations on their lists, they may feel tremendous relief or that their burden has been lifted. For others, that feeling may not come until later. It is common for many to feel as though nothing has changed. But the reality is, everything has changed. God has heard your prayer, and the freedom process has been activated. To solidify what you have just done, the next step is critical.

MEMORIALIZE THE ACT

Forgiving someone is an important step, and it is critical for you to remember that you did it. That may seem odd to say that you would forget doing this, especially since it was so hard to do in the first place. But the reality is—we do "forget." We'll explain this in a moment. But in the meantime, take out the sheet of paper on which you wrote the names of those you wanted to forgive. In a prominent place, on that sheet of paper, write the date and time of when you finished your forgiveness prayer. It will look like this:

My Forgiveness List
(Today's Date)
I have made the decision to forgive the following people:

- Judy—Stole my watch—*(Today's Date)* at 7:35 P.M.
- James—Broke my heart—*(Today's Date)* at 8:15 P.M.
- Justin—Doesn't support his child—*(Today's Date)* at 8:27 P.M.
- Daddy—What he did to Mama—*(Today's Date)* at 9:30 P.M.
- That man who rear-ended my car last month while talking on his cell phone—*(Today's Date)* at 9:53 P.M.
- Tina—The girl who always teased me in junior high school —*(Today's Date)* at 10:00 P.M.

The reason it's important to write down the date and time is because you will need to remember the exact moment that you forgave the person when what they did to you suddenly pops back into your mind. Let me give you an example from my own life that happened some years ago.

There was a woman—let's call her Dana—who I thought was my friend. One evening Dana informed me that since my boyfriend and I had split up three weeks earlier, she really liked him *and* she was going to do whatever it took to get him. She was "sorry" if that hurt me, but that's just the way it is . . . BAM! I was so stunned, I didn't really say anything to her at the time. Within a couple of weeks, they hooked up—for a short time. I wasn't really mad at him, because we had already broken up. Plus, my expectations of him were pretty low anyway. But Dana really hurt my feelings. She violated the unwritten Girlfriend Code that you don't just up and date my ex-man when it's still fresh! I was angry, felt betrayed, and was very bitter.

Every day I thought about Dana and my ex-boyfriend. I thought about how she told me she was going to go after him. I rehearsed different scenarios in my mind about my reaction to what she said. The scenes varied. Sometimes I kickboxed her in her gut, wiping that little smirk off her face. Other times, it was just a simple slap across her betraying face. What I imagined was much more satisfying than the reality of what had really occurred. I tortured myself by fantasizing about them having fun together, laughing, going places, and kissing each other! But mostly I was angry. I relived my whole rela-

163

tionship with her—remembering the nice things I did for and with her. Each time the fantasy ended with her betrayal. Because I continued to relive the incident in my mind, the wound stayed fresh . . . even after a year. One day while I was talking to a friend about that incident (again), she gently told me that it sounded like I was bitter and I needed to move on with my life. She continued by saying that I needed to forgive Dana and let it go. At first I was angry with her for saying that. Me . . . bitter? But I was bitter. Then I thought, "So what if I was bitter—Dana dogged me out!" But the bottom line was that I was living in the past and I was stuck.

I had no choice. I had to forgive her. I needed to get over it and move on. I said a simple prayer similar to the one suggested in this chapter, and I wrote down the time and date. That was actually the easy part. The hard part came later. Because I was so used to thinking about her betrayal, even though I had forgiven her, those thoughts still came back. The very next day, I found myself standing in the bathroom thinking about what Dana said, how she said it, and getting angry all over again. I started imagining a new, more expressive response to her announcement. Just as I was getting into my grudge-laden fantasy, I heard a small, gentle voice say,

"I thought you forgave Dana last night."
"I did!" I replied.
"Doesn't sound like it . . ."
(Long pause) "So what do I do with these thoughts?"
"Take a stand against them . . . recall that you forgave her."

From that point forward, whenever I began to rehearse what she did to me, I would say aloud:

"I forgave Dana on August 17th at 4:37 P.M. In the name of Jesus, I will not continue to rehearse this experience in my mind!"

Then I would purposefully change my thoughts to something else. Sometimes the desire to rehearse the wrong would leave—other times it seemed to put up a fight. It's amazing how persistent these types of repetitive thoughts can be. I remember a couple of days later, yet again, I found myself reliving the Dana experience. I said my statement about forgiving Dana—but less than two minutes later the thoughts came back. I did it again. The thought immediately came back again. That afternoon, I must have said, "I forgave Dana on August 17th at 4:37 P.M." literally sixty or seventy times. Even months later, the thought would try to creep back, but I just repeated that I forgave her, and the thought eventually left.

I have shared this experience to give you encouragement. If the repetitive thoughts keep coming back, that's absolutely natural. After all, it had become a habit. But it is a habit that can be broken. Keep on repeating that you forgave that person with the date and the time. It's not about "forgive and forget"; it's about forgiving until you are no longer in prison. Never give up—keep fighting until you truly escape that prison.

Lastly, when you make the *decision* to forgive, your *feelings* don't always cooperate. You don't feel like forgiving. But one day, after the stage of fighting the repetitive thoughts, the feelings eventually follow. One day, you will feel so free, and you will know in your heart that you have truly forgiven the person of that wrong. God wants you to be free.

It is for freedom that Christ has set us free. Stand firm, then, and do not let yourselves be burdened again by a yoke of slavery.
(Galatians 5:1)

24

I'VE BEEN BETRAYED: I HAVE A RIGHT TO BE BITTER

Bitterly she weeps at night,
tears are upon her cheeks ...
All her friends have betrayed her;
they have become her enemies.
—LAMENTATIONS 1:2

BETRAYED

Doris and Elaina had been best friends since college and remained roommates even after they graduated seventeen years ago. Doris is a thirty-seven-year-old human relations director who had been praying to get married for the last twelve years. Doris's dream of marriage was finally coming true when she met Greg, who was introduced to her by her sister's husband. Within seven months, they were engaged and had set their wedding date for the following July. Doris was very pleased that Elaina liked Greg too. Greg was the first boyfriend that Elaina seemed to approve of.

About four months into Doris's engagement, she went out of town on a business trip. Because Greg didn't really want her to go, she made a point of finishing up her appointments quickly to race home and surprise him a day early. Really, Doris was the one who was surprised when she walked in on Elaina and Greg in bed together. Doris immediately severed both relationships; she broke off her engagement and moved in with her mother. Doris was betrayed by her fiancé and her best friend. However, a year later Doris still feels stuck. She realizes that her whole life changed that fateful afternoon, but she feels that more was lost than two important relationships—a part of herself is now missing. But what part? She's not sure.

THE INTIMACY OF BETRAYAL

Betrayal is a major cause of bitterness. Betrayal occurs when someone we trust has done or said something that hurts us physically, emotionally, or spiritually, and their action (or inaction) results in our being unable to trust them or ourselves. Betrayal can happen through a direct action, such as revealing a secret (purposefully or inadvertently), infidelity, disloyalty, exposing a weakness, ridicule, or deceit. But betrayal can also occur as a result of a failure to act, like not protecting or standing up for someone.

Betrayals happen when those we trust don't show fidelity to us. Fidelity is a character quality that embodies faithfulness, commitment, and loyalty. Fidelity is present when someone else is looking out for your best interests; it is important in all relationships, not just in a marriage or a parent-child relationship. Our heart's desire is for fidelity. We want our family to be loyal, our friends trustworthy, and those we date to be faithful. Fidelity is held in high regard, and we have a natural desire to want to trust others. We yearn to be with people with whom we can let down our guard, and we desire relationships wherein we are accepted with all of our flaws and weaknesses. We want our secrets kept, our bodies safe, our things to stay in our possession, and our families intact. These are our expectations for our family, friends, coworkers, fellow church members, and romantic interests. We want to be safe. Is that too much to ask?

According to *Webster's Ninth New Collegiate Dictionary,* the word *betray* comes from a French word *tradere,* which means traitor or to hand over or deliver. When someone betrays us, he or she may "hand over" to another more than just our secrets, for example. Much more is lost as a result of the act of betrayal. Our expectation of safety, whether emotional or physical, is snatched away. Our trust, faith, and innocence are also stripped from us. When we are betrayed, we lose:

- our ability to trust people,
- our faith in our own judgment, and
- our innocence about the motives and intentions of others.

Doris said that she had lost more than just her relationship with her fiancé and her best friend; she also lost a piece of herself. That's exactly what occurred. She lost her ability to trust, her faith in others, and her innocence. Those three intangible ingredients help to make us who we are. To be betrayed is so very painful because we lose so much of ourselves. Betrayers must be incredibly evil people to do such mean-spirited things, right? Well, not necessarily.

THE BETRAYER

What kind of person is a betrayer? The truth is any one of us can betray someone else. We may have betrayed someone in the past, and it's entirely possible that we will betray in the future. We think we don't betray others, but because betrayal can be subtle we may not always recognize it. We can betray someone by sharing her secret with a girl-friend. How many times have we started conversations with, "Girl, you can't tell a soul, but guess what So-and-So told me." We may have betrayed someone's trust by dating their boyfriend, by not defending a friend when she needed us to stand up for her, or by lying to her. All of those examples are betrayals of one degree or another.

Betrayal is also subjective. While we may consider someone's action to be a betrayal, the other person involved may not realize he has betrayed us. One reason for that is because we each have different life experiences, values, and ethics which ultimately shape our character. Our character colors our expectations, and betrayal is connected to our expectations. If we are expecting faithfulness from a person who does not have that quality, then eventually we will be betrayed. If we're expecting safety from someone who is a violator, we will be betrayed. If we're expecting honesty from someone who lies, we will be betrayed. If we're expecting loyalty from someone who is out for themselves, we will be betrayed. This is why it is so important to recognize another person's values, because it gives us opportunity to discover their character. But other ingredients also play a role in betrayal, such as:

- Anger
- Alcoholism and drug abuse
- Greed
- Jealousy or envy
- Hatred
- Psychological or emotional problems
- Desperate need for money
- Revenge
- Love

A betrayal comes to mind which happened to me several years ago. I had a few friends over to my home for a girls' night. My purse was in my bedroom, and my wallet was just lying on my bed. After everyone left, I noticed that my wallet was open and thirty dollars was missing. I had the expectation that none of my girlfriends would steal from me. I know who did it; she never confessed, but it altered our friendship permanently. I felt betrayed. My girlfriend, on the other hand, was not an evil person, but it came out later that she had a drug problem.

We betray because it is part of our sin nature. We were born with the desire to look out for our own interests and not the interests of others. The Bible describes the depths to which we humans are capable of committing betrayal:

Brother will betray brother to death, and a father his child; children will rebel against their parents and have them put to death.
(Matthew 10:21)

Betrayal is a natural stepping-stone to bitterness. We have discovered that betrayal occurs when someone we trust has done or said something that hurts us. We also know that our expectation of being safe emotionally or physically is stolen from us when we are betrayed, plus we have lost our ability to trust others and ourselves. The bottom line with betrayal is that our hearts have been broken. Because of our previous experiences, it's tough to believe that God wants to heal our hearts. But can He really heal us?

CHAPTER
25

FREE YOURSELF FROM TRAPPED THINKING: GOD CAN'T HEAL MY BROKEN HEART

*See to it that no one misses the grace of God
and that no bitter root grows up
to cause trouble and defile many.*
—HEBREWS 12:15

Most of us know what it's like to have our heart broken. A broken heart can be the result of an unfulfilled dream, a severed relationship, unmet expectations, or a few harmful words directed toward us. The experience of a broken heart is both painful and perplexing. Our hearts feel the pain and our minds are perplexed. For those of us who have experienced a broken heart, even this description may seem insufficient.

The word *heart* in the New Testament (*kardia*) and in the Old Testament *(leb)* have much in common. They both describe our heart as being the deep part of who we are. Our heart is our core: our center, the seat of our will, desires, and emotions. Therefore, when our heart is broken, the pain runs deep. Painful experiences can cause our heart to feel crushed, torn into pieces, or even destroyed. As a result, we begin to question ourselves, others, and God. We ask, "Why didn't God keep me from going through all this trouble?"

When we have a broken heart, we feel as though we will never recover because that part of us cannot be fixed. When most things break, we know exactly what to do; we either fix or replace the items. If our car breaks down, we take it to a mechanic. If our computer goes haywire, we call the "help" line. If a fingernail chips, a quick trip to our manicurist can have it replaced within minutes (at any length we desire). However, a broken heart is very different; we can't get a quick fix. We want to find out how to stop the pain. Usually when a heart is broken it turns bitter, which leads to trapped thinking. When our heart is wounded, we can easily become trapped into believing that:

- the pain will never go away, or
- God can't heal my heart.

Yes, a broken heart hurts. It's painful, and if the truth be told, many times we don't deserve it. But guess what. God can do great things with a broken heart. He takes extreme pleasure in repairing that which we think is irreparable. He takes tenderhearted care in comforting the parts of us we feel cannot be comforted. Most of all, He will heal our hurting heart if we will bring the broken parts of our being to Him.

See if you can imagine God writing the following letter to you concerning your broken heart:

Dear Daughter:
    I know your heart is hurting, and I see that your spirit has been crushed. I feel your pain, and I want you to know how much I care about you. My main concern, however, is for you to know that I understand your pain, and I want to heal your heart. I am your Father, and I can heal you. All I want for you to do is to give Me your problems once and for all and let Me take care of the rest. You see, when you give Me your problems, that's when I can heal your broken heart and replace it with a joyful spirit. As a matter of fact, I want to mend all your wounds. Please under-stand that when I see you with a broken heart, I see it as an op-portunity to get closer to you. Will you come closer to Me?
                                            Your Father who loves you

What an exciting letter! Was it difficult to imagine God saying those words to you? You don't have to imagine this letter because God has addressed these very words to you through His Scripture. Take a look at the three verses used to create this letter of comfort:

Cast all your anxiety on him because he cares for you.

(1 Peter 5:7)

He heals the brokenhearted and binds up their wounds.

(Psalm 147:3)

The Lord is close to the brokenhearted and saves those who are crushed in spirit.

(Psalm 34:18)

The promises in these Scriptures are clear and true. God wants you to give Him all that concerns you because He cares for you. He wants to bind up your wounds like a loving parent who would bandage their child's cuts to ensure proper healing. Finally, God wants to use your broken heart as an awesome opportunity to get closer to you and to heal your spirit.

Your heavenly Father expects your hurting heart to be fully restored. He wants to transform your brokenness into a blessing. However, in order for you to move from being trapped to transformed, you must give your broken heart to Him by seeking Him with all your heart (Psalm 119:2), no matter what condition it's in.

26

TRUSTING AGAIN: LEARN TO BEAT BETRAYAL

Though you have made me see troubles,
many and bitter, you will restore my life again;
from the depths of the earth you will again bring me up.
—PSALM 71:20

THE IMPORTANCE OF TRUST

God wants us to be able to exercise our ability to trust. Trust is a key ingredient in developing gratifying relationships on every level, whether it be with friends, children, or coworkers. Unfortunately, as we experience more betrayal in life, it becomes increasingly difficult to take chances on trusting again.

Trust is also a critical ingredient needed in order to develop a healthy relationship with God. As a general rule, the more we trust God, the more confidence we have in being able to depend on Him. The less we trust Him, the less likely we are to have assuredness that He will meet our needs. Here are just a few examples where God encourages us to trust Him:

Trust in the LORD with all your heart and lean not on your own understanding; in all your ways acknowledge him, and he will make your paths straight.

(Proverbs 3:5)

They cried to you and were saved; in you they trusted and were not disappointed.

(Psalm 22:5)

May the God of hope fill you with all joy and peace as you trust in him, so that you may overflow with hope by the power of the Holy Spirit.

(Romans 15:13)

Those who know your name will trust in you, for you, LORD, have never forsaken those who seek you.

(Psalm 9:10)

Trust is like an onion in that trust is built in layers. At its core, trust is the ability to rely on someone other than yourself. It is the fundamental belief that the person you believe in will come through for you. Trust is built in layers because we start first by just sharing a little bit of ourselves. As we see how the other person handles that, we add a layer by sharing more of ourselves. Trust definitely includes the feeling of safety, and that sense of security is one that is established over time. It is the peace that you feel when it is safe to share every area of who you are.

Critical to beating betrayal is learning how to trust again. There are two basic segments needed to rebuild trust. First, it is important to *"look back."* That means that you examine the betrayal and deal with it. The next segment is to *"move forward."* This entails laying a strong foundation inside yourself that will enable you to have trust in your future relationships. Let's start by looking back.

LOOKING BACK

Looking back is an important part of healing. Unless we take a look at our past, we cannot take the steps needed to change our future. We begin by changing how we look at our past. Bitterness, however, is not resolved in three or four quick and easy steps. Peeling back the layers of hurt, misunderstanding, humiliation, lies, and shame takes time and a commitment to yourself. The following are suggestions on how to begin the process. And with all processes that involve healing, allow yourself time.

Talk About It

If you have an unresolved issue of betrayal, it is important to begin to talk about and share your experience. Talking about the incident with someone who doesn't make you feel ashamed or blamed is a great healer. However, if the betrayal involved trauma, we highly recommend talking with a professional who can walk with you through the process. Other safe places to talk about betrayal may be with a pastor, with lay counselors, in a women's group, at a trauma counseling center, or in a recovery group. Freedom comes from talking about the betrayal. The longer we keep these feelings bottled up inside of us, the more power the betrayal has over us and the greater impact it has on our life. Talking loosens betrayal's grip on your life, eventually forcing it to release you.

Weigh the Value of the Relationship

When you are betrayed, a major question that needs to be resolved is whether or not you want to continue to have a relationship with the betrayer. If you do continue having a relationship with him, determine what type of relationship it will be. Can the relationship be salvaged, or do you want to jettison the betrayer out of your life? The following practical questions can help you with the decision-making process:

1. How were you betrayed? Be specific about what they did.
2. On a scale of 1 to 10, what kind of relationship did you have with the betrayer? (1 = barely knew the person; 10 = intimate friendship, parental relationship, or marital relationship.)
3. On a scale of 1 to 10, how did the betrayal affect you? (1 = a mere annoyance; 10 = physical injury to yourself or someone else.)

4. Before the betrayal, how did the "betrayer" make you feel about yourself? For example, did you feel competent, positive, encouraged or did they make you feel ashamed of yourself, inept, guilty?
5. Before the betrayal, did he or she encourage you toward your goals or did he or she ridicule your dreams?
6. What kind of memories do you have about your relationship together? Are they happy? Sad? A little bit of both?
7. Do you have a desire to maintain a relationship with them? If so, will it be different?

Once you think through your answers, then you can move forward to the next step: making the decision about discussing the situation with the betrayer.

Confront the Perpetrator
There are several decisions that you must make for yourself before confronting a betrayer. The first and most important decision is:

"Is it safe for you to confront them?"

If it is not safe for you to do so, DO NOT CONFRONT THEM. If you are not placed in a threatening situation, you then must decide if you want to expend the emotional energy needed to confront someone. If you have already decided that you do not want to salvage the relationship, or if you do not have a desire to discuss the betrayal with them, then there is nothing that says that you should. Confronting a betrayer is purely a personal decision. However, confronting the betrayer can be quite helpful because it will allow you to get some things off of your chest. Here are some tips:

• Make an appointment to discuss the problem. Choose a time when you will not be interrupted.
• Stick to the subject. Do not start with small talk. Get right to the point of the meeting.
• Plan what you're going to say—even if that means that you have to write it out.
• Describe how the event made you feel. No one can dispute

your feelings because they are YOUR feelings. For example, "I felt angry and hurt because you lied to me." They cannot challenge the fact that you felt anger or that you were hurt because that is how you felt.

- Use "I" words, not "you" statements. Rather than saying, "You did this to me . . ." say something like, "When this happened, *it made me feel unwanted.*"
- Lower your expectations. Depending on the personality of the perpetrator, you may never get an apology or any admission of guilt. Think through in advance how you will feel and react if no apology is forthcoming.

Release the Betrayal

A good friend of mine led a discipleship group in which each member was recovering from some sort of emotional betrayal. The group had the most wonderful "release ceremony." They went to the beach and told one another what they wanted to get out of their lives. They went around the circle so each woman could individually share what she wanted to release; then the group prayed for her and she surrendered her betrayal to God. One by one, as each woman surrendered her betrayal and received her prayer of release, she let go of her helium-filled balloon. The balloon symbolically carried away the betrayal and took it up to God. There was something emotionally healing about watching the balloon float up to the heavens until it was out of sight. You may want to make a beautiful memory with a good friend as you symbolically "release the betrayal."

MOVING FORWARD

Our future is in front of us, and to live it fully, we have to move forward. There is a season for looking back, but the season for moving forward is the longer and can be the more exciting of the two seasons. Here are some things that can help you move forward with your life.

Improve Your Judgment

One of the qualities that is commonly stolen from us after being betrayed is our ability to trust our own judgment. Many times we blame ourselves for missing red flags in relationships or allowing ourselves to become involved with certain people.

Here are some steps to help you begin to trust your own judgment again.

- *Surround Yourself with Wise People*—Think about people whom you know that have demonstrated an ability to make good decisions—perhaps it's an older woman, a married couple, or a girlfriend that you know. Invite two or three of these people into your life to teach you how to do the same. God encourages us in His Word to do that very thing:

> *The lips of the righteous nourish many, but fools die for lack of judgment.*
> (Proverbs 10:21)

> *For lack of guidance a nation falls, but many advisers make victory sure.*
> (Proverbs 11:14)

> *Plans fail for lack of counsel, but with many advisers they succeed.*
> (Proverbs 15:22)

- *Create a Set of Rules for Yourself*—Learn a lesson from the betrayal. Make sure that you grow wiser as a result of what has happened. Sit down and write out all the things you have learned, like what to look for in a true friend or in a dating relationship. Write out a positive description of the type of friends you would like to have in your life. When you meet someone who could be a new friend, pull out your list of desired qualities, and see how they compare. Ask yourself if they are the type of person that you need in your life. If so, get to know them better and recheck your list at a later date to make sure things are still on track. If you find that they are not enhancing your life, you may want to discuss your concerns with them and/or choose to move on. Creating a set of rules to live by can help you make good decisions.

Also, revisit and revise your rules from time to time. As you think of new character traits that you admire, add those to your list. There may also be some things that you may want to remove from your list. Keep in mind that this list is not meant to leave you without choices; it is only to be used as a road map to travel by.

- *Repeatedly Read the Book of Proverbs*—Proverbs gives wisdom for practical everyday life. For example, it warns us about the dangers of co-signing. One common way that we are betrayed is by co-signing for someone else (Proverbs 17:18). When you co-sign, the creditor doesn't even have to look for the debtor, but can come directly after you for payment. All you need to feel betrayed is one phone call from a creditor asking you to immediately pay the debt of a friend or a family member for whom you co-signed. Proverbs warns us repeatedly not to co-sign for someone else. The book of Proverbs also gives us advice on the type of friends to have, the kind of people to avoid, and what to do with our money. It is fascinating reading.

- *Ask God to Give You Wisdom*—God is eager to give us wisdom, and He invites us to ask.

If any of you lacks wisdom, he should ask God, who gives generously to all without finding fault, and it will be given to him.
(James 1:5)

God is, after all, our best source of wisdom. Just ask Him for it.

Trust Someone
Take a chance and trust someone. How do you do that? By taking baby steps. When you want to draw closer to someone but feel a bit hesitant to trust again, try sharing a small piece of information with her and see how she handles it. Is she open or closed? Is she accepting or judgmental? If she handles that well, share something else and see what she does with it. Give her bits and pieces of who you are to see how she handles it. Does she appreciate you? If so, you may have met a new friend. Also, keep in mind that she is

taking baby steps to trust you also. Treat her the way you desire to be treated.

Learn to Trust God

Trusting human beings will never be problem-free. Why? Because we are imperfect and are bound to make mistakes. Your emotional and spiritual foundation is to be in God. We can learn to trust God by turning our hearts toward Him. Jeremiah 17:5–6 says:

> This is what the LORD says: "Cursed is the one who trusts in man, who depends on flesh for his strength and whose heart turns away from the LORD. He will be like a bush in the wastelands; he will not see prosperity when it comes. He will dwell in the parched places of the desert, in a salt land where no one lives."

When we dwell in bitterness, we are already living in the "parched places of the desert." In bitterness, we are isolated and alone; therefore we already reside "in a salt land where no one lives." As we turn our hearts toward God and make those baby steps in learning to trust in Him, God is faithful to open our eyes so that we will see "prosperity when it comes."

Take those steps away from bitterness. Start by looking back. Talk about the betrayal. Decide if you want to continue the relationship. If so, determine the type of relationship you want. Confront the betrayer, but only if it is safe for you to do so. Release the betrayal through forgiveness, and then move forward with your life.

CHAPTER
27

BITTER STICKS
AND STONES:
THOSE WORDS
DID HURT ME

Each heart knows its own bitterness.
—PROVERBS 14:10

When growing up, I was very thin and was constantly teased about being skinny. One evening when I was about nine years old, we had just finished eating some barbecue and we were collecting rib bones to give to the dog. Someone was walking around with a paper bag saying, "Bones for the dog—Bones for the dog . . ." Someone else said, "Val, jump in." Everybody had a good long laugh. Over thirty years and sixty pounds later, I can still hear the laughter and feel a twinge of the anger.

Growing up can be tough. All of us have been laughed at, teased, or have been the object of a joke. We can have amazingly clear memories of childhood taunts that can still make us cringe decades later. Words can hurt us, and sometimes they leave permanent emotional scars. Teasing and constant criticism are two types of experiences many of us have endured which have resulted in bitterness and low self-esteem.

WHEN SOMEONE HAS SOMETHING TO SAY

Teasing and constant criticism damage our views of ourselves. These two types of communication bring up feelings of resentment and bitterness when we think back over our life. Teasing is when someone uses humor to pick at someone else's weaknesses in order to shame or humiliate them. Linda Sones Feinberg, the author of *Teasing: Innocent Fun or Sadistic Malice,* did a wonderful search into the meaning of the word *tease.*

> "Tease" comes from the old English word *"taesan"* which was used, about the year 1000, to mean "pluck, pull apart." Three hundred years later the word *tesien* appeared, with the meaning to "separate the fibers of, shred, or card" (wool or flax). Before 1325 the word had become *"tesen."* The transferred sense of "to vex or worry, annoy," appeared in 1619, and "the sense of one who teases" is first recorded in Dickens's *Bleak House* (1852).[1]

Teasing hurts. Many of us have been the victims of merciless teasing. Much of the teasing we have experienced most likely happened during our formative years—between elementary and high school. We could be teased about anything that someone else thought was unique or different about us, like our height, weight, the shade of our skin, our hair, legs, voice, nose, clothes, or being poor or wealthy. Anything was fair game when a teaser's interest was piqued. Teasing is very big in the African-American culture. Although there is a very fine line, some teasing is good-natured; but it's the hurtful teasing that can cause bitterness.

Teasing also includes calling each other names and, unfortunately, some of those names have stuck with us. There are many childhood nicknames which are remembered by old friends and family members that we would rather they forget. We could get these names in a variety of ways. Some nicknames like Chubby, Cakey, Fatty, Stretch, Tiny, Lips, or Sweet Pea were a result of physical characteristics; other names may describe a temperament like Slow Poke or Pokey. Many names describe athletic abilities like Speed or Bullet. Some names described our standing in the family like Trey, Junior, Baby Girl, and the like. Some nicknames are relatively harmless while others have shaped how we look at ourselves. Often our self-esteem has been injured through teasing or nicknames that we didn't like. When we were pulled apart and ridiculed for things over which we had no control, it caused us frustration, tears, bitterness, and, in particular, a lowered estimation and appreciation of ourselves.

Constant criticism is another way that we are verbally pulled apart. Criticism occurs when someone finds a fault in us and tells us or others about it. To be criticized is not necessarily a bad thing. Some criticism is good and can help us improve. When the criticism is presented with kindness, it makes it so much easier to accept. What we are talking about is the type of fault-finding criticism that is continuous and ongoing. The criticizers, many times, are family members like parents who desire for us to improve or siblings with the motive to annoy or irritate. This was the case with Eartha.

THE GREAT ESCAPE

Eartha loves living in Boston because it puts her over 900 miles away from her family who have been a constant source of criticism. When she thinks back on her childhood and teenage years, all she remembers her parents saying to her was:

"Try harder; don't be so lazy."
"If you lost some weight, you could run faster."
"Why can't you be more like everybody else?!!"

Eartha, named after Eartha Kitt, the talented multilingual dancer/actress, was the third of four children born to athletic parents. Her mother was an avid tennis player, and she passed that talent along to Eartha's bubbly older sister, Nia. Her father was an ex-player in the old ABA league, the rivals of the NBA, and went on to be a coach at a local college. Her older brother, Jimmy, inherited his Dad's quickness and is now playing ball in Italy. Eartha's younger sister, Bridgette, is a college track star with the goal of competing in the Olympics. The whole family lives and breathes sports—everyone except Eartha.

Eartha is serious, solitary in nature, and a devourer of books. Reading books satisfied her curious mind; but mostly, they helped her to mentally escape her family. Eartha was usually curled up in a quiet corner reading—much to the consternation of her parents. To make matters worse, everyone else in the family had a thin-to-medium build, but not Eartha. She was pleasingly plump while growing up and now she was just heavy. Both Nia and Bridgette had flawless skin and shoulder-length hair, but Eartha's skin was prone to break-out and her hair just would not grow past the tops of her ears. Eartha's mother used to constantly lecture her about the importance of losing weight, exercising, and being more appealing. Jimmy and Bridgette teased her mercilessly, calling her Mother Earth, Big Bertha, or Wide Berth. Only Nia would stand up for her, telling the others to leave her alone. She was the one person in her family who didn't tease or criticize her but encouraged her. Eartha believes that she would have gone crazy if Nia hadn't been around to support her.

Fortunately, Eartha always did well in school. By the time she graduated from high school, she already had a full academic scholarship to attend a prestigious women's college outside of Boston. After graduating, Eartha received a job offer in Boston which she accepted. Free of her family, she built a new life that excluded them. But Eartha is filled with self-doubt—she relies on others to tell her if she has done a good job. She feels reserved and insecure—always striving to prove that she's good enough because deep down inside, she doesn't believe that she is. Eartha is bitter, and her self-esteem is at an all-time low.

BITTERNESS AND CRITICISM

We grow bitter when we get tired of being picked on and criticized. If we continually get the message that "we're just not good enough," it impacts our self-worth. Throughout our childhood, we look for approval from a relatively small circle of people that surround us: our family, a circle of friends, and our teachers. If there is a consistent air of disapproval and fault-finding, with an absence of encouragement and concerted effort to build a child's self-concept, by the time he or she reaches her critical teen years, she can be withdrawn or rebellious.

Not only have many of us received the "not good enough" message from our home life, but that same message is received by African-American women on a daily basis from our society. For example, we do not fit the American standard of beauty, which is being tall and thin with long blonde hair. Whenever we look at television, read magazines, or even pass billboards, we see the images of how women "should" look. As a result, of all the racial groups in the United States, African-Americans buy one out of every five cosmetics sold and one out of every three hair products sold.[2] We have spent billions on beauty.

Living with the conclusion that "we're not good enough" causes us to lower our expectations and induces us to settle. As a result, we don't dream big dreams and expect them to come true. Maybe we don't finish school; perhaps we give up too easily when we are met with the normal resistance that comes when we strive to better ourselves. We accept people and situations that are not good for us. We allow ourselves to become involved with men who just want to have sex with us and don't want to marry us. We allow folks into our lives who continue to tear us down and not build us up. All of this occurs because our own idea of ourselves, our uniqueness, and our intrinsic value have been lowered. We don't value ourselves. The bitterness resulting from constant criticism contributes to a harmful outlook that says "I don't like myself."

When we are bitter toward ourselves, we treat ourselves just like we would treat someone else with whom we are bitter. For example, when we are bitter with someone else, we criticize them. We do the same thing to ourselves. We agree and repeat what we've heard said about us. That's when we start saying things to ourselves like: I am clumsy, I'm stupid, I'm ugly, my behind is too big, my legs are too thin, my hair looks bad, etc. It's emotionally draining being bitter and angry at "who" we are. Because we disapprove of ourselves, it's easy to believe that God disapproves of us also . . . but nothing could be further from the truth.

28

FREE YOURSELF FROM TRAPPED THINKING: GOD DISAPPROVES OF ME

*Accept one another ... just as Christ accepted you,
in order to bring praise to God.*
—ROMANS 15:7

As you discovered in chapter 27, constant criticism and teasing over many years directly affect what we think and believe about ourselves. When we are the recipients of continual put-downs, the fundamental message that is finalized in our minds is that we are flawed. This message travels deep inside of us. When we believe we are flawed, it feels as though something is wrong with us. It is an overall belief that we are faulty or defective. Once we are convinced we are flawed, it affects our worldview—how we see and interpret the world around us. Everywhere we go, not only do we feel as though we are "less than," but we begin to believe that others see our shortcomings as well. We second-guess if others like us. We wonder if God approves of us. After all, those who teased us did not approve of us, so why should anyone else . . . including God?

THE PROBLEM WITH BEING PICKED ON

Once we come to the conclusion that the very essence of who we are is damaged, a natural human response is to do one thing: to find ways to prove to ourselves and others that nothing is wrong with us. We set up our lives in such a way that our behavior is out to prove that we are OK. Instead of feeling comfortable with who we are and accepting all parts of ourselves (the good, the bad, and the ugly), the never-ending experience of winning the approval of others takes over. Here is a list of things that we do to gain the approval of others and to feel good about ourselves:

- **Perfectionism**—*If I can only get everything right and not make any dumb mistakes, I will be acceptable.*
- **Focus on Appearance**—*If I always look flawless, no one will see my faults.*
- **Religious Activity**—*If I can only read my Bible and pray enough, then God will approve of me.*
- **Pleasing Parents**—*If I can be what my parents want me to be, then they will approve of me.*
- **Buying Friendship or Love**—*If I spend enough money on others, my gifts to them will make me acceptable in their sight.*
- **Promiscuity**—*If I have sex with him, maybe he'll love me.*
- **Self-Correction and Criticism**—*If I can stop this bad habit, then God will accept me.*
- **Educational Achievements**—*If I can only pass this exam, I will prove my worth or value and others will like me.*

In order to recognize that we may be living an approval-seeking lifestyle, we must slow down, spend time in prayer, be willing to examine ourselves, and ask God to change us. Slowing down puts us in prayer position. Prayer is the ultimate position of humility. It gives us opportunity to speak to God and allows Him to speak to us. As we prayerfully examine our hearts, God is always willing to reveal what is there and direct us toward change. Once we identify the ways in which we are seeking approval, then we can begin to accept God's approval.

PROMISES OF APPROVAL

The belief that God does not approve of us can be subtle, but the results can send us on a never-ending quest for peace and approval. However, one of the most fundamental and freeing messages in the Bible is that we embrace the fact that we are fully loved, accepted, and approved by God. Once we accept this promise, we have less of a need to seek the approval of those around us.

It is important to know that God approves of us in order to live a successful life that is pleasing to Him. According to Galatians 1:10, when we live our lives with the goal to please others, it becomes impossible to serve God:

Am I now trying to win the approval of men, or of God? Or am I trying to please men? If I were still trying to please men, I would not be a servant of Christ.

Free yourself from seeking the approval of others by accepting the fact that God already approves of you—flaws and all. Do this by replacing what others have told you about yourself with the true promises of God's approval that are listed below:

Accept one another, then, just as Christ accepted you, in order to bring praise to God.

(Romans 15:7)

But God demonstrates his own love for us in this: While we were still sinners, Christ died for us.

(Romans 5:8)

But because of his great love for us, God, who is rich in mercy, made us alive with Christ even when we were dead in transgressions—it is by grace you have been saved.

(Ephesians 2:4–5)

And you also were included in Christ when you heard the word of truth, the gospel of your salvation. Having believed, you were marked in him with a seal, the promised Holy Spirit, who is a deposit guaranteeing our inheritance until the redemption of those who are God's possession—to the praise of His glory.

(Ephesians 1:13–14)

Who shall separate us from the love of Christ? Shall trouble or hardship or persecution or famine or nakedness or danger or sword? As it is written: "For your sake we face death all day long; we are considered as sheep to be slaughtered." No, in all these things we are more than conquerors through him who loved us. For I am convinced that neither death nor life, neither angels nor demons, neither the present nor the future, nor any powers, neither height nor depth, nor anything else in all creation, will be able to separate us from the love of God that is in Christ Jesus our Lord.

(Romans 8:35–39)

Read these promises once a day to know in your spirit that God approves of you and loves you. Building on the knowledge of God's love is the foundation for building your self-esteem. But what are the other steps? What other things can be done to increase our worth in our own eyes?

29

REBUILDING
SELF

The wise woman builds her house,
but with her own hands the foolish one tears hers down.
—PROVERBS 14:1

BUILDING YOUR HOUSE

Building your self-esteem is a lot like constructing a house. It's very systematic. First, you look to build your house on a strong foundation, and that foundation is the knowledge of God's love and acceptance of you. After the foundation is laid, then the walls are erected, and finally you put on the roof. Proverbs says that it is a wise woman who builds her house, and it's a foolish one that tears hers down. We tear down our house when we criticize ourselves and think poorly of who we are. We saw in chapter 27 how the words of others impact our estimation of ourselves. We also discovered that when others tease us or when we are in an atmosphere of constant criticism, the value of our own self-worth is lowered. Teasing and constant criticism is when *others* are trying to tear down our house. *We* tear down our own house with our guilt, shame, and self-loathing.

In the last chapter, we saw that God does not disapprove of us in the way we or others have expressed disapproval. In fact, we uncovered that God does not disapprove of us at all. Since we now know this, we can begin to build our self-esteem on the sound foundation that God loves and approves of us. We are going to do this by employing the "3 Cs": *commitment, connection,* and *community.*

COMMITMENT

It takes commitment to yourself to build your self-worth. You have to decide if it is important for you to put forth the effort needed to restructure your self-concept. This decision is something that only you can make for yourself—even God can't make it for you. But once you decide this is what you want, God is standing right there to help. You are making the commitment to be loving, gentle, and compassionate to yourself. Until you learn to love yourself, it is almost impossible to truly show love to someone else. In Mark 12:31, it says that we are to love our neighbor *as we love ourselves.* If we loved and treated others the way we treat ourselves, they would run from us. Therefore, we must learn to love and appreciate ourselves, allowing God to love us also; then His love that He pours into us can spill out of us onto others. In order to do this, our esteem must be intact.

The first step to learning how to love ourselves is to discover why we feel poorly about ourselves. This is done by pinpointing those things that have caused us to feel bad.

Identifying the Negative Messages
Take a piece of paper and write down the parts of yourself that you feel bad about. Take your time and think about those things. Then write down a list of your responses to each of the following questions:

- What have you been teased about?
- What are you ashamed of or what regrets do you have when you think about your life?
- What do you dislike about your body?
- What decisions have you made that you do not like?
- What have others criticized you about?

• What have you failed at or what parts of your life do you perceive to be a failure?

Make your list as complete as possible. For some this exercise could take about twenty to thirty minutes; for others, it may be longer. The main idea is to complete the task and discover yourself. You want to identify as many negative messages as possible that others have said to you and that you have said to yourself.

Forgiving Yourself

As we saw in chapter 23, forgiveness is a decision. This is true whether you are forgiving someone else or yourself. You have to decide that you want to stop punishing yourself—for past decisions, how you look, or the things that you are ashamed of. Follow the steps outlined in chapter 23 that explain how to forgive others, and apply those steps to forgiving yourself. Take a look at the things on your list, and purposefully forgive yourself of the items listed. Below is an example of a prayer of self-forgiveness:

Dear heavenly Father:

I have made the decision to forgive myself for (<u>you name it</u>). I have decided to no longer be that foolish woman who tears down her house that You mentioned in Proverbs 14:1. Instead, I choose to be wise and build my house by showing myself the love and forgiveness I deserve. You have forgiven me of my sins; therefore, it is wrong of me not to forgive myself. I surrender these feelings to You because they are a burden and a weight. In Matthew 11:28–29, You invite all who are weary and burdened to come to You, and You will give them rest. In the name of Jesus, I want to get rid of this burden of thinking badly about myself. I am tired of tearing myself down. I desire to take Your yoke and to learn from You so I can find rest for my soul. I desire to be set free from the bitterness that comes from not accepting myself. Therefore, as an act of faith, I ask You to heal my heart and my mind this day.

In Jesus' name.

Use this prayer, or make up one of your own. The important thing is to get rid of the baggage that you have been carrying of the things that you have been holding against yourself.

Accepting Yourself

An important ingredient in forgiving yourself involves accepting yourself as you are. There are some things that I have learned to accept about myself. For example, I know that I'll probably never be athletic, nor am I supermodel material. But so what! There are plenty of things I do like about myself. I'm funny—I might not be able to make anyone else laugh, but I can crack myself up; I'm a good friend; and I have an excellent sense of direction—I rarely get lost. Building your esteem is about learning your strengths and acknowledging your weaknesses. It's human to have weaknesses. Just have the same compassion for yourself that you would have for someone else.

Another part of accepting yourself is learning to understand yourself. Discover the way you think and notice how you react in different situations. Learn your own emotional vulnerabilities. Discover what kind of comments irritate you. Then think of alternative ways to respond. Become a student of yourself.

Reprogram Yourself

Many times we live our lives on cruise control. When certain things happen, we automatically start demeaning ourselves. Go back to your list of negative messages and make up a new message to counteract the original negative messages. For example:

Negative Message: "I'm too old."
New Message: "I'm the age I'm supposed to be right now."

Negative Message: "My rear end is too big."
New Message: "I am shapely."

You get the idea. Write down a positive statement to yourself for every negative one on your sheet. Repeat your statement every time your negative message comes to mind. You have to continuously counteract your negative messages with your new positive statements. Be committed to being consistent. And as you do, you will gradually see a change in your self-talk—those things that you say to yourself. You may also want to repeat all your positive statements to yourself twice a day: when you get up in the morning and before you go to sleep at night. This process helps you to embed the positive message in your mind. Building your self-esteem is all about being gentle and loving with yourself.

CONNECTION

The next step in our "3 C" recipe for self-esteem is "connection." It is necessary for us to be connected with others. We all need support when we embark on something as challenging as building our self-esteem. God directs us not to do things alone. Even Jesus, when He was here on earth, had a group of twelve that surrounded Him as He did His work. In Ecclesiastes 4:9–12, it says:

Two are better than one, because they have a good return for their work: If one falls down, his friend can help him up. But pity the man who falls and has no one to help him up! Also, if two lie down together, they will keep warm. But how can one keep warm alone? Though one may be overpowered, two can defend themselves. A cord of three strands is not quickly broken.

Share what you are doing with a friend. Choose someone who is empathetic to your challenge. Find someone who will encourage you to keep going as you go through the natural highs and lows that are usual for life.

COMMUNITY

The final "C" in the "3 C" formula to building your self-esteem is "community." The goal of self-esteem is not just to build up yourself, but to build up others as well. We want to encourage you to give yourself to others. Help someone else. We all have so much to offer one another; that's why God put us all together and has obligated us to have contact with one another. As you give to others, not only will your self-worth increase, but your feelings of compassion will grow. You will possess more love and grace for others.

197

We hear it all the time. There are three character qualities that men say they have a hard time finding in women today:

- a woman who is compassionate—one who can empathize, come alongside, and help alleviate pain or stress,
- a woman who is loving, and
- a woman who is not bitter—whose heart has not grown cold because of experiences in life.

Compassion and a loving attitude are qualities that men find highly desirable in a wife. And those are the same qualities that God looks for in His servants. It is that loving compassion that will drive us to reach out and help others. It is the absence of bitterness that allows us to take emotional risks with others. The desire to help others in their struggles, the urge to help alleviate someone else's pain, the longing to encourage others along the way—that is the kind of heart God is looking for in His people. God honors that attitude and He will honor you.

God is not unjust; he will not forget your work and the love you have shown him as you have helped his people and continue to help them.

(Hebrews 6:10)

EPILOGUE—
BEST WISHES

Although this book has come to an end, your ongoing journey with God is just beginning. It has been our prayer that some of the suggestions and ideas in this book will challenge your thinking about God and your circumstances. God wants to set you free of spiritual, mental, and emotional burdens that have hindered you in the past. And He starts this process by challenging our thinking. Lightening loads and leaving burdens behind don't happen overnight. Some pretty tough things, like forgiveness, have been brought up in these pages. Therefore, give yourself time.

Take advantage of this season of singleness, knowing that you are whole and complete just as you are and that it is a lie if someone tells you otherwise. This is the time to get to know and appreciate yourself and the God who created you. Take the time to fall in love with God and you will fall in love with life. God will help you to discover and pursue your purpose, and along the path He has for you, the Lord will take care of the deep desires of your heart. Therefore, don't be anxious for anything, but instead give every concern and request to God. When you do that, the peace of God which surpasses all of our understanding will guard your heart and your mind in Christ Jesus (Philippians 4:5–7).

Respectfully,
Valerie and Jerome

PLAN OF SALVATION

The most important decision that you make in your life is to choose to accept God's offer to have a relationship with Him. He extends a personal invitation to each of us to have an intimate relationship with Him. We all need to be connected to God, because without a relationship with Him, we are totally separated from Him. It is our natural human nature that disconnects us from God because we are sinners. The Bible says in Romans 3:23:

For all have sinned and fall short of the glory of God.

It doesn't matter how good you believe you are, what wonderful things you do, or how many millions of dollars you give away to do noble things. Nor does it matter how long you have been in church, taught Sunday school, or if *you* were christened as a baby. If you do not have a relationship with God, none of that matters. This means that you remember a specific point in time where *you* (*not* your parents or your grandmama) accepted Jesus as your Lord and Savior. Good works don't matter, because no matter how wonderful our works are, our very nature—the essence of who we are—is permeated with sin. It is that sin that eternally separates us from God.

But God prepared a way for us to have our sins forgiven (Romans 5:8). His Son Jesus came to earth with the mission and purpose to die for us as a perfect sacrifice to atone for our sins (2 Corinthians 5:21). He was our substitute. The Bible says that the true and just payment for sin is death (Romans 6:23). That's why someone had to die to pay for our sins, and that is what Jesus did. He paid the penalty for our sins with His life so that we could be reunited with God. But we have to make two decisions. The first one is to agree with God that we are sinners (Acts 17:30), and the second is that we accept what Jesus has done for us. But there is more . . .

Jesus was a sinless man who bore all of the sins of mankind when He died on the cross. He allowed His life to be taken; He died and was buried in a tomb. On the third day, Jesus was resurrected from the dead. Many witnesses saw Him, spoke to Him, and ate with Him. At one point, over 500 people saw Him at one time. Later, He rose straight up into heaven where He is seated (Hebrews 12:2) at the right hand of God making intercession for us (Hebrews 7:25 KJV).

Today is the best day to make the decision to accept what Jesus has done on our behalf, because tomorrow is not promised. Don't put it off thinking that you have to "clean up your act first." The whole point is that we can't clean up our act. We must become "born again." Our very sin nature keeps us in bondage. Instead, allow God to give you new life (John 3:3–8). Besides that, there is nothing that we can do to *earn* salvation. Ephesians 2:8–9 says:

> For it is by grace you have been saved, through faith—and this not from yourselves, it is the gift of God—not by works, so that no one can boast.

God promises that *whoever* calls on Him for salvation, He will accept them as His children (Romans 10:13). It doesn't matter what you've done or where you've been. There is *nothing* that you have done in your life that God will not forgive (Colossians 1:13–14). He always forgives (Psalm 103:2–4). Romans 10:9–11 tells what we must do to be saved:

> If you confess with your mouth, "Jesus is Lord," and believe in your heart that God raised him from the dead, you will be saved. For it is with your heart that you believe and are justified, and it is with your mouth that you confess and are saved.

As the Scripture says, "The one who trusts in him will never be put to shame" (Romans 9:33).

Heavenly Father:
You have promised not to reject me if I come to You, so I do so right now. I open my heart to You in the name of Jesus. I confess that I am a sinner, but this day I choose to accept what Jesus did on the cross. I believe He took my place, and He died for my sins so that I may be forgiven by You. He shed His blood, died, was buried, and was resurrected again. He is now seated in heaven at Your right hand. I accept what He did in my place, and this day I declare that Jesus is my Lord and Savior. He saved me from eternal death and delivered me from spending eternity in hell, forever separated from You. But because Jesus is now my Savior, I have everlasting life, and when it comes my time to die, I believe that I will be with You in heaven. This day I give my life to You. I invite You to come into my life right now. I thank You for Your mercy and Your grace.

Congratulations! You have just taken the most important step that will change your life for all eternity. God loves you, dear one. He wants you to get to know Him. He wants you to know that He hears you when you pray. God will begin to draw you close to Him. Find a church where you are taught the Word. Ask people around you to recommend a Bible-teaching church that teaches in a loving and encouraging manner.

We pray for God to keep and protect you . . . which He has already promised to do.

In Jesus' name,
Jerome and Valerie

NOTES

INTRODUCTION

1. *2001 The New York Times Almanac;* edited by John W. Wright, Penguin Reference; New York; 2000; 278 (Note: Only people 18 years or older included in statistic—Source: U.S. Bureau of the Census, Statistical Abstract of the United States.)

CHAPTER 2

1. Gary C. Collins, *Overcoming Anxiety* (Santa Ana, California: Vision House, 1973).
2. Betsy Cohen, *The Snow White Syndrome: All About Envy* (New York: MacMillan Publishing, 1986), xiii.
3. William F. May, *A Catalogue of Sins: A Contemporary Examination of Christian Conscience* (New York: Holt, Rinehart and Winston, 1967), 78.
4. Helmut Schoeck, *Envy: A Theory of Social Behaviour* (Indianapolis: Liberty Press).
5. Joseph H. Berke, *The Tyranny of Malice: Exploring the Dark Side of Character and Culture* (New York: Summit Books), 19.
6. Helmut Schoeck, *Envy: A Theory of Social Behaviour* (Indianapolis: Liberty Press), 3.

CHAPTER 3

1. Poker is a gambling card game that involves deception and is played in rounds—the number of times around the table. To start the game, each player puts in a sum of money to start the jackpot. To stay in the game the player must continue to "ante up," or "fold"

and be out of the game. When the gambler chooses to ante up, it means that he puts in additional money to stay in the game. If a player has a good hand, enough money, and the pot is enticing enough, generally, he will continue to ante up. Deception is involved when a player's hand may not be so good but he wants another player to think it is better than it is to win the pot. Therefore, it is to the bluffer's advantage to ante up with confidence, thereby increasing the stakes and making the decision for the next player harder to make. The pot is won if everyone else folds or the game is called. If everyone folds, then the winner does not have to show his hand. If the game is called, the cards are compared and a winner is decided based on his cards. Poker has led to the death of many gamblers.

CHAPTER 7

1. William F. May, *A Catalogue of Sins: A Contemporary Examination of Christian Conscience* (New York: Holt, Rinehart and Winston, 1967), 78.
2. Ibid., 73.

CHAPTER 10

1. *Webster's Ninth New Collegiate Dictionary,* s.v. "discouragement."

CHAPTER 17

1. *Webster's Ninth New Collegiate Dictionary,* s.v. "passive."

CHAPTER 21

1. *The American Heritage Dictionary of the English Language,* 4th ed., s.v. "prison."

CHAPTER 27

1. Linda Sones Feinberg, *Teasing: Innocent Fun or Sadistic Malice* (Far Hills, New Jersey: New Horizon Press, 1996), 5.
2. Earl Ofari Hutchison, "In Search of Unnappy Hair" (*The Black World Today*, 10/2/1999).

Other Great Titles from Lift Every Voice

Planting Seeds of Hope

How To Reach A New Generation of African Americans with the Gospel

African American youth are looking for role models they can trust. The network of support is already in place. God has placed many of His most compassionate workers among today's African American young people. This book is written to help youth workers, pastors, parents and others who care about reaching young people with the hope of the Gospel.

ISBN: 0-8024-4197-1

God Just Showed Up

God Just Showed Up is a compilation of various short stories written by 19 talented writers and Christian educators on their personal experiences of how God changed their lives. Included is the life story of Curtis Martin who before being known as a running back for the New York Jets football team, and the NFL 1995 Rookie of the Year, lived in fear of not reaching his 21st Birthday because of the violence in his life, and how God changed his life.

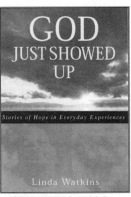

ISBN: 0-8024-6591-9

Taking Care of Business

Establishing A Financial Legacy for the African American Family

Most people wrongly believe that the money they earn belongs to them, and they have a right to do with it as whatever they please. However, the Biblical view of stewardship involves both ownership and accountability. Lee Jenkins guides us in setting goals in the areas of family, faith, friends, finance and fitness. In addition to providing guidance and direction, he reviews goals that make us think strategically.

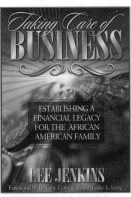

ISBN: 0-8024-4016-9